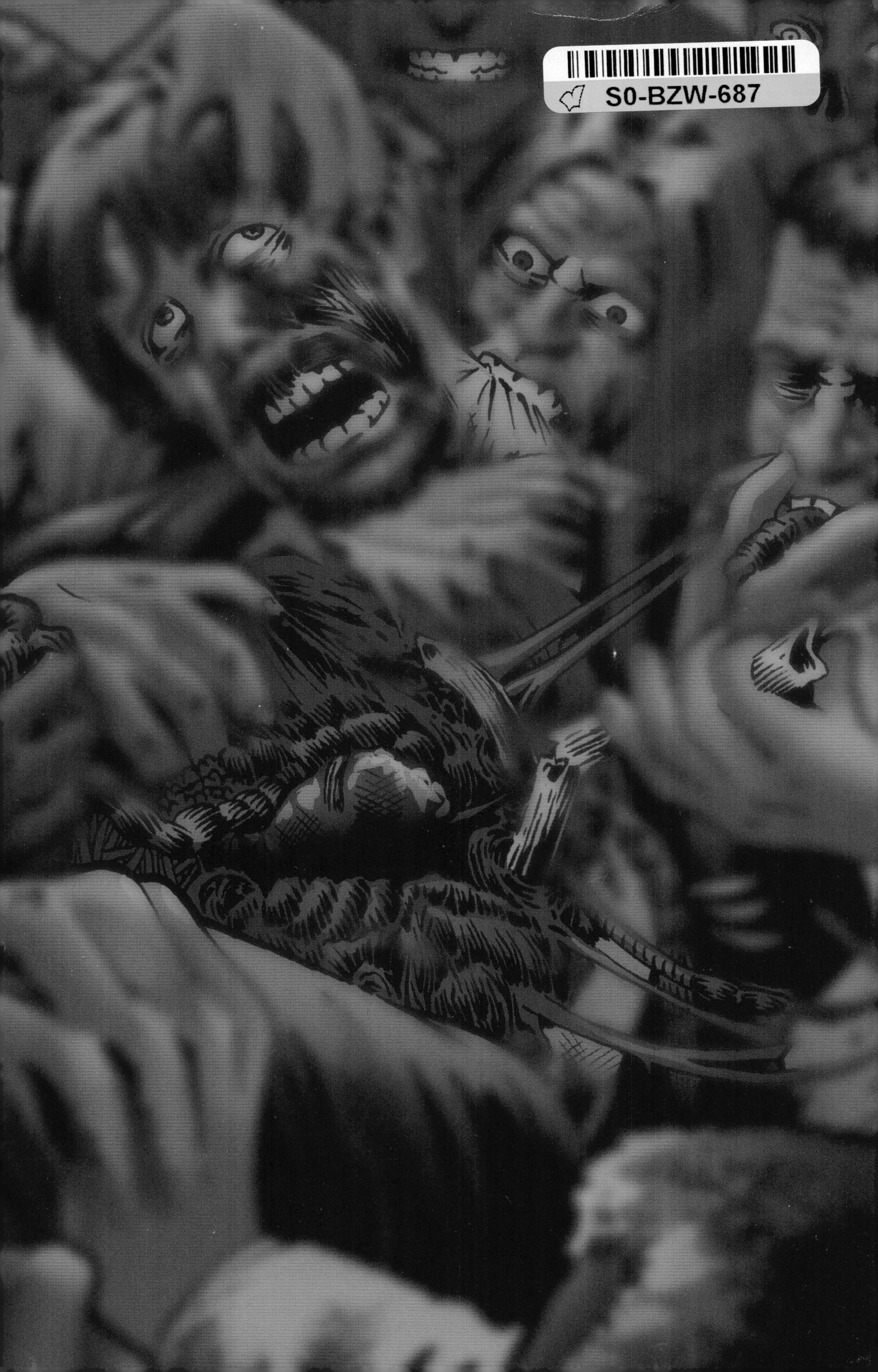

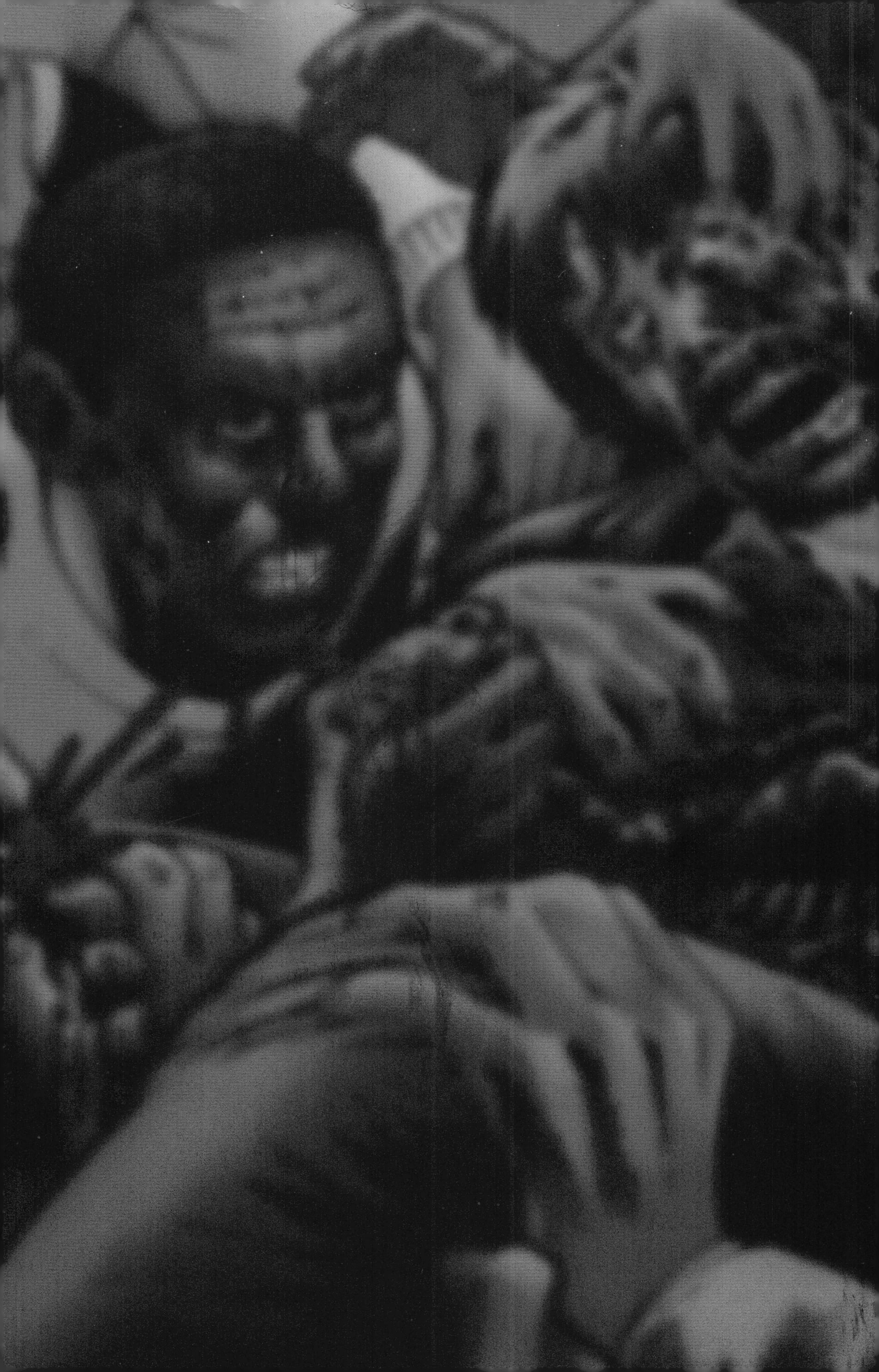

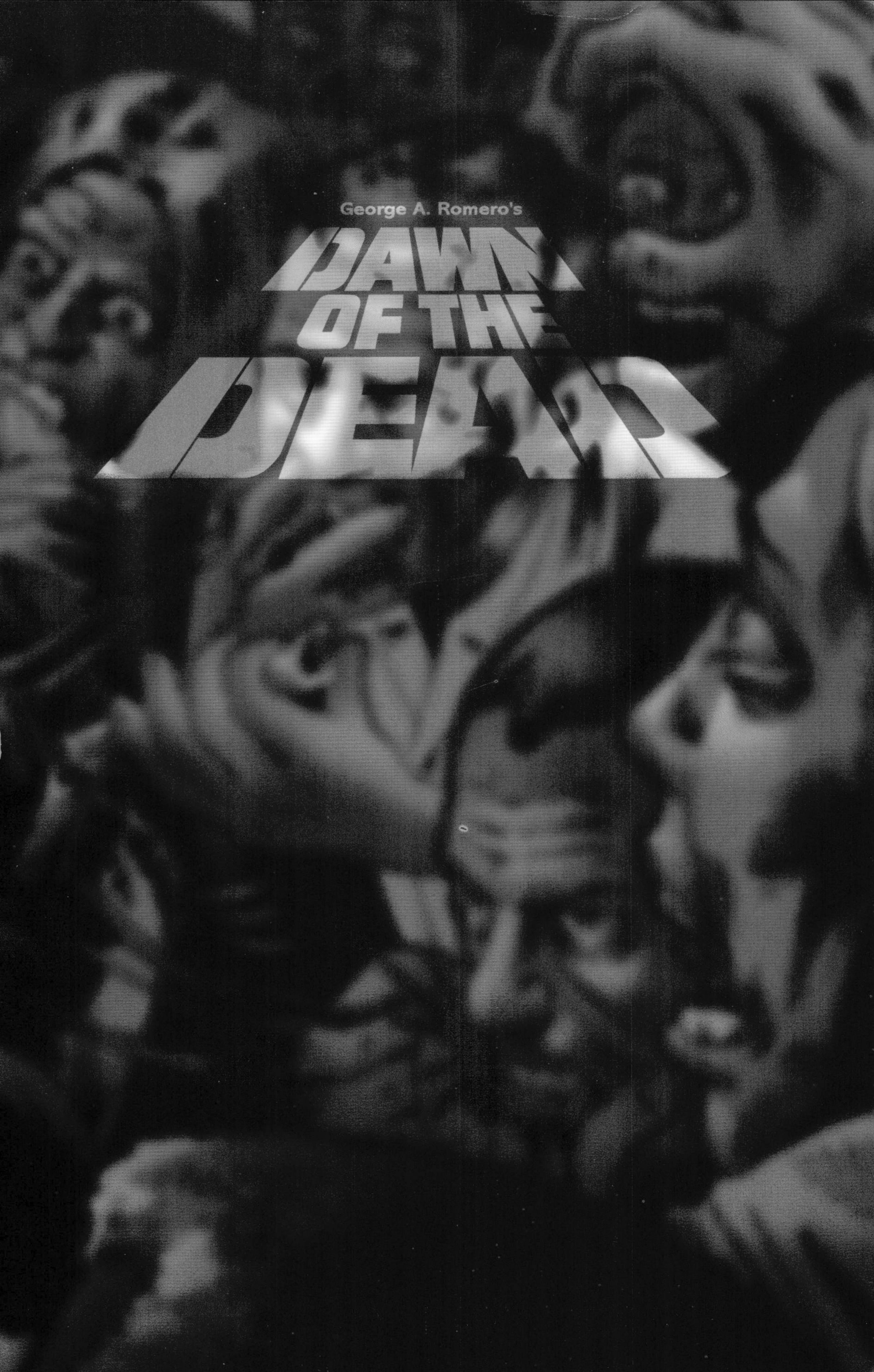
George A. Romero's
DAWN OF THE DEAD

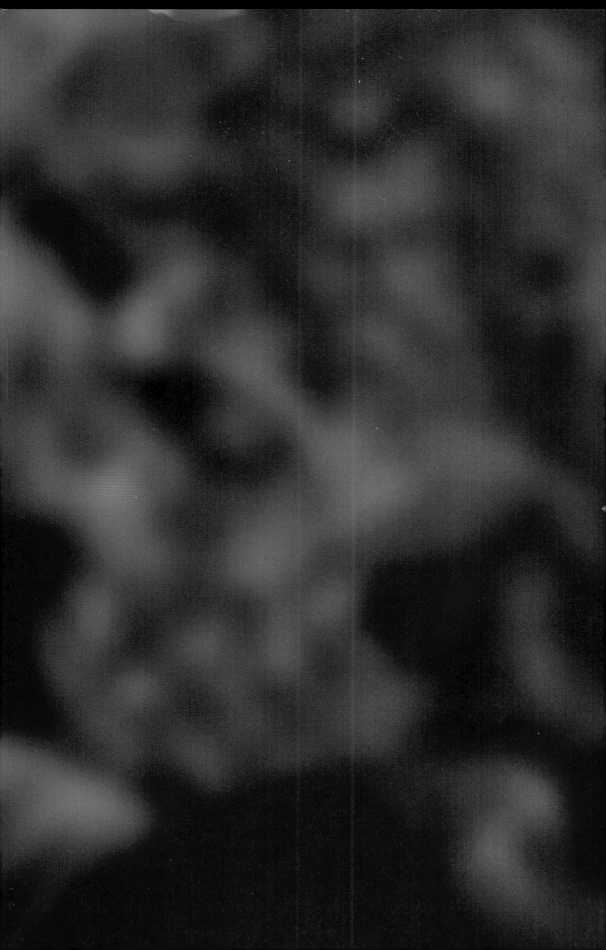

George A. Romero's

DAWN OF THE DEAD

Steve Niles   Chee   Tom B. Long

www.idwpublishing.com

ISBN: 1-932382-32-1
07 06 05 04   1 2 3 4 5

Ted Adams, Publisher
Chris Ryall, Editor-in-Chief
Robbie Robbins, Design Director
Kris Oprisko, Vice President
Alex Garner, Art Director
Cindy Chapman, Designer
Beau Smith, Sales & Marketing
Chance Boren, Editorial Assistant
Jeremy Corps, Editorial Assistant
Yumiko Miyano, Business Development
Rick Privman, Business Development

Adaptation:
Steve Niles

Pencils and Inks:
Chee

Colors:
Tom B. Long

Lettering and design:
Robbie Robbins

Design Assistant:
Cindy Chapman

Original Series Editor:
Jeff Mariotte

Editor:
Alex Garner

Cover Photos:
Katherine S. Kolbert

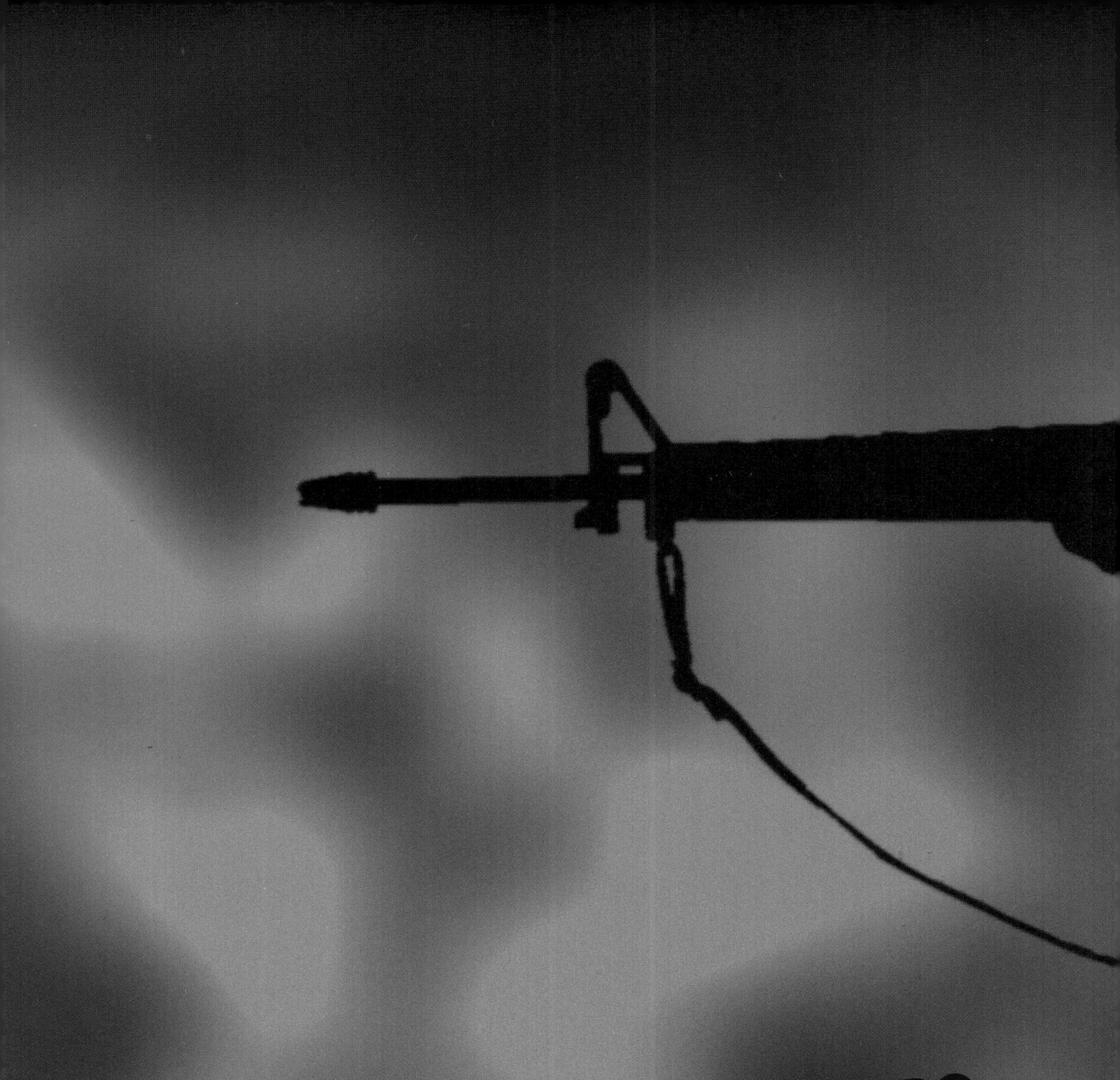

INTRODUCTION BY GEORGE A. ROMERO

First let me say that I love Steve Niles's adaptation of *Dawn of the Dead* for IDW. Comic fans and movie fans alike, especially fans of my film version of *Dawn*, have a treat in store when they open these pages.

Shooting the original film was grueling. The cast and crew worked their butts off, all at night, after Monroeville Mall had closed for business, for thirty-five nights. While the schedule was exhausting, and we faced enormous production difficulties, all of us gleefully knew that we were making exactly the movie we always hoped it would be, a balls-out horror flick with lots of socio-political satire.

On all the films we worked on together, Richard P. Rubinstein was a generous producer who protected my creative controls and basically let me get away with murder. In that

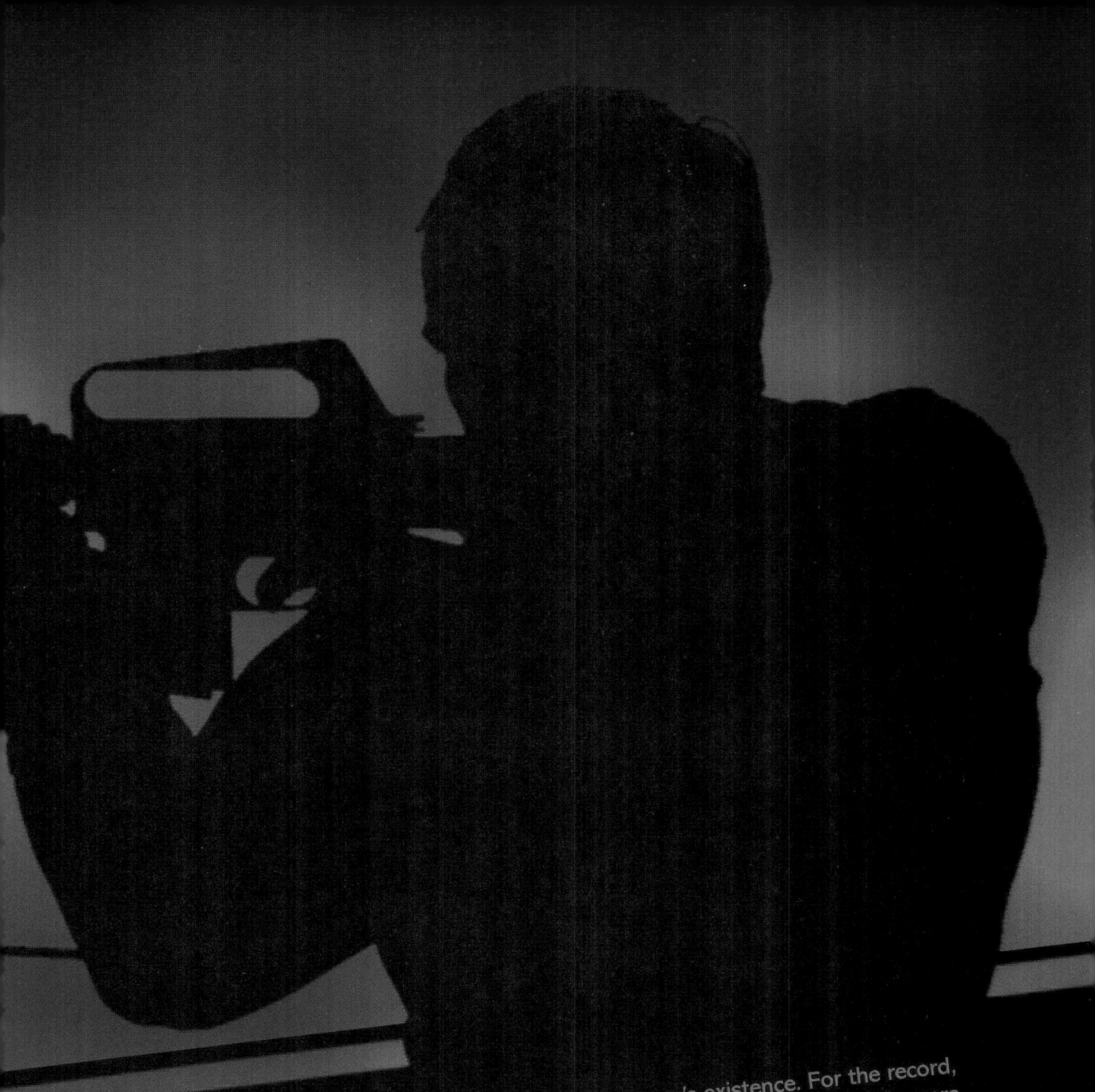

sense, he deserves as much credit as I for the original *Dawn's* existence. For the record, I liked the remake Richard produced. When I conceived the original, indoor malls were rare and new. Now they have become part of everyday life, so satire is lost. I also cannot adjust to fast-moving zombies. In my mind, they, as the Sheriff said in the original *Night of the Living Dead*, should be "…dead…all messed up." Despite those reservations, I think Zack Snyder's version of *Dawn* is a hot, satisfying thriller that respects not only the original film but also the entire genre. I'm sure Richard deserves much of the credit for that as well.

Naturally, my heart remains true to the original, to that good time we had, despite exhaustion, to Ken, Scott, Gaylen and David, to Savini and Gornick, and all the dedicated artists who invested the time and gave so much of themselves in order to bring my ideas to life. So I am delighted to see that original version of *Dawn* come to life again. My thanks to Steve Niles, Chee, Tom Long, Ted Adams, Jeff Mariotte, Robbie Robbins, and Mike Messina at New Amsterdam for a terrific job. Readers who know the film are bound to love the comics, as I do. Newcomers will now have a chance to read my original story. Thanks for bringing it to them. Thanks for keeping the dead alive.

George A. Romero
2004

Original cover of *Dawn of the Dead* issue 1

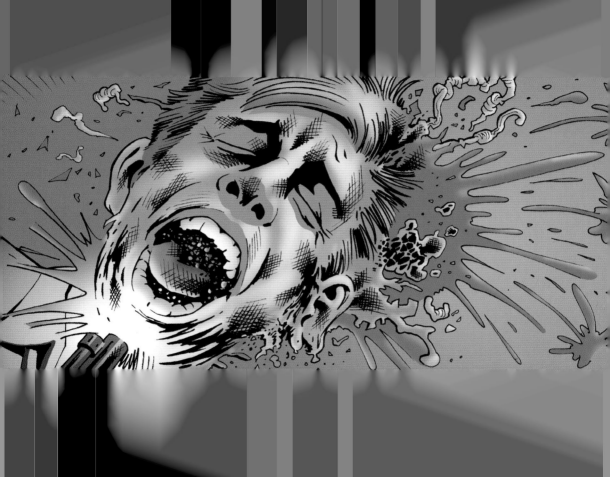

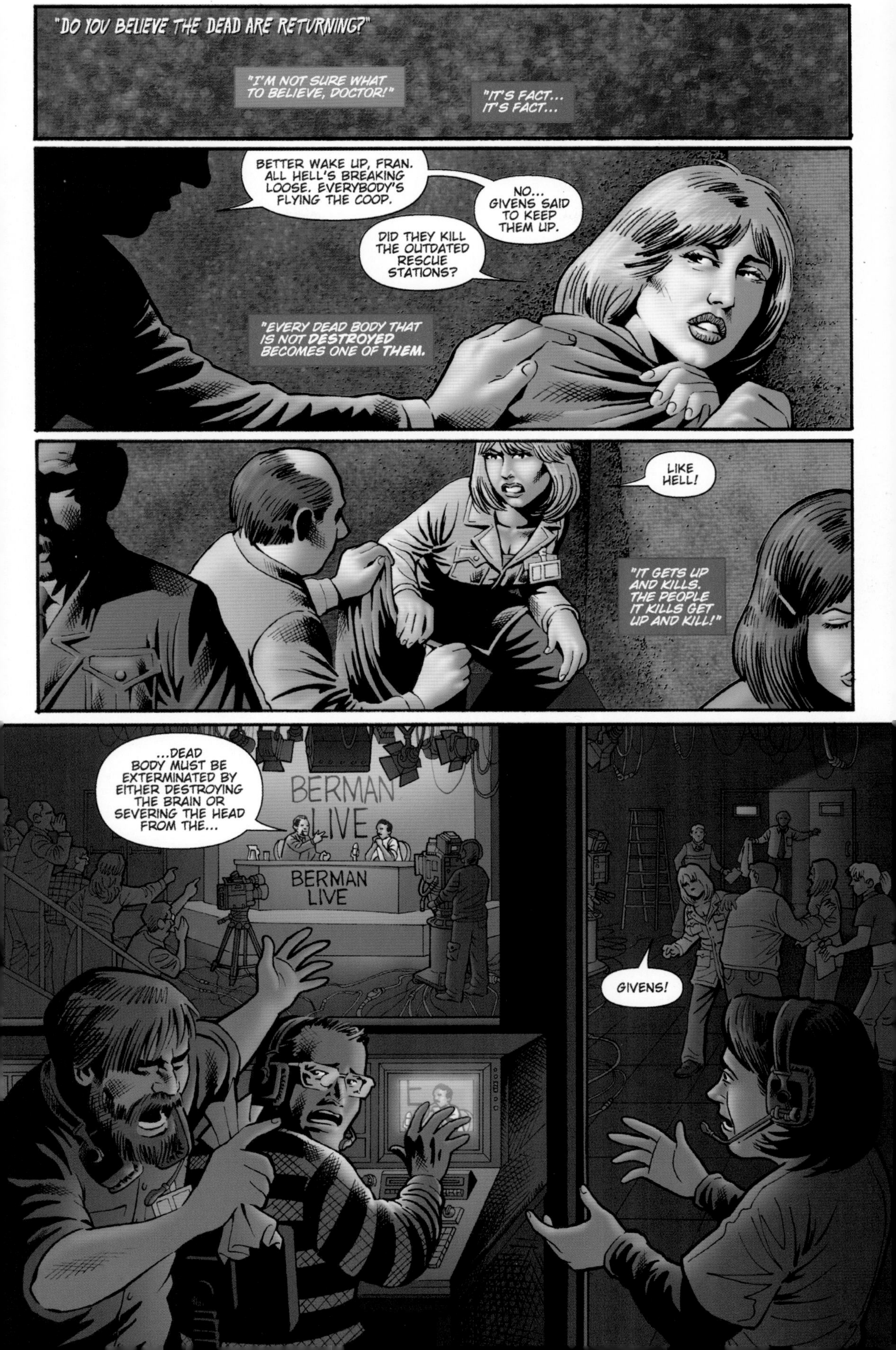
"DO YOU BELIEVE THE DEAD ARE RETURNING?"
"I'M NOT SURE WHAT TO BELIEVE, DOCTOR!"
"IT'S FACT... IT'S FACT...
BETTER WAKE UP, FRAN. ALL HELL'S BREAKING LOOSE. EVERYBODY'S FLYING THE COOP.
NO... GIVENS SAID TO KEEP THEM UP.
DID THEY KILL THE OUTDATED RESCUE STATIONS?
"EVERY DEAD BODY THAT IS NOT DESTROYED BECOMES ONE OF THEM.
LIKE HELL!
"IT GETS UP AND KILLS. THE PEOPLE IT KILLS GET UP AND KILL!"
...DEAD BODY MUST BE EXTERMINATED BY EITHER DESTROYING THE BRAIN OR SEVERING THE HEAD FROM THE...
BERMAN LIVE
BERMAN LIVE
GIVENS!

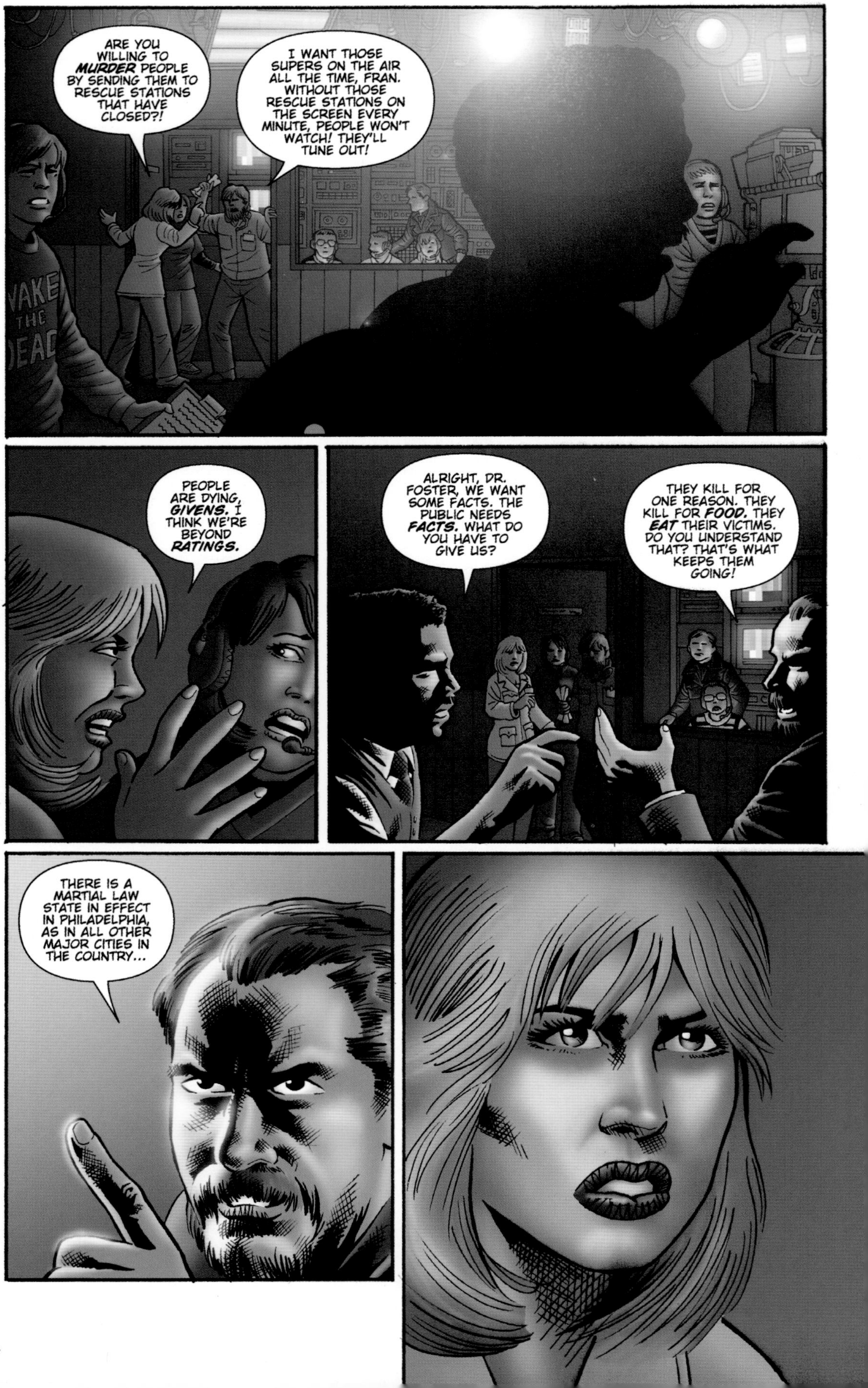
ARE YOU WILLING TO MURDER PEOPLE BY SENDING THEM TO RESCUE STATIONS THAT HAVE CLOSED?!
I WANT THOSE SUPERS ON THE AIR ALL THE TIME, FRAN. WITHOUT THOSE RESCUE STATIONS ON THE SCREEN EVERY MINUTE, PEOPLE WON'T WATCH! THEY'LL TUNE OUT!
WAKE THE DEAD
PEOPLE ARE DYING, GIVENS. I THINK WE'RE BEYOND RATINGS.
ALRIGHT, DR. FOSTER, WE WANT SOME FACTS. THE PUBLIC NEEDS FACTS. WHAT DO YOU HAVE TO GIVE US?
THEY KILL FOR ONE REASON. THEY KILL FOR FOOD. THEY EAT THEIR VICTIMS. DO YOU UNDERSTAND THAT? THAT'S WHAT KEEPS THEM GOING!
THERE IS A MARTIAL LAW STATE IN EFFECT IN PHILADELPHIA, AS IN ALL OTHER MAJOR CITIES IN THE COUNTRY...

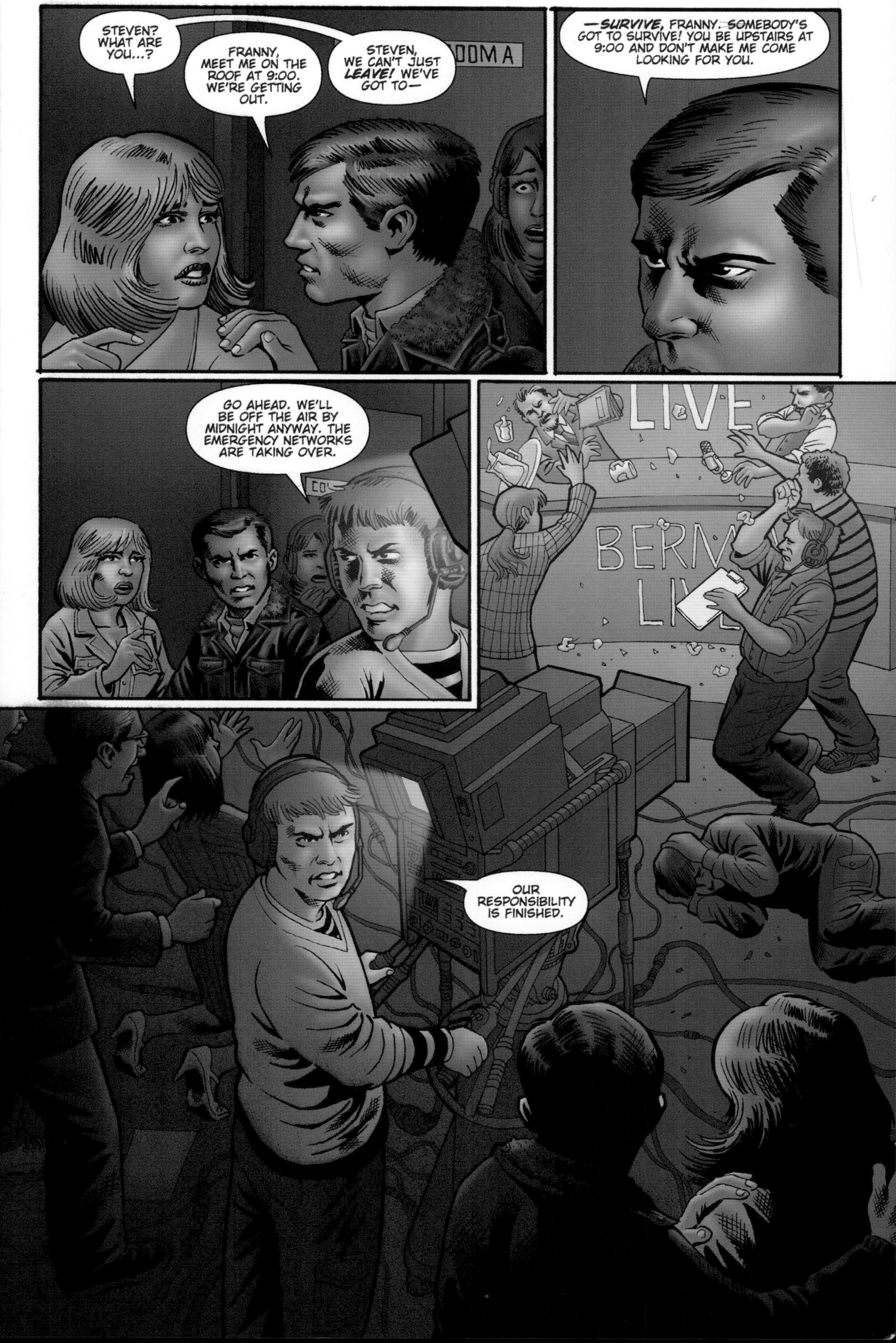
STEVEN? WHAT ARE YOU...?
FRANNY, MEET ME ON THE ROOF AT 9:00. WE'RE GETTING OUT.
STEVEN, WE CAN'T JUST LEAVE! WE'VE GOT TO—
—SURVIVE, FRANNY. SOMEBODY'S GOT TO SURVIVE! YOU BE UPSTAIRS AT 9:00 AND DON'T MAKE ME COME LOOKING FOR YOU.
GO AHEAD. WE'LL BE OFF THE AIR BY MIDNIGHT ANYWAY. THE EMERGENCY NETWORKS ARE TAKING OVER.
LIVE
OUR RESPONSIBILITY IS FINISHED.

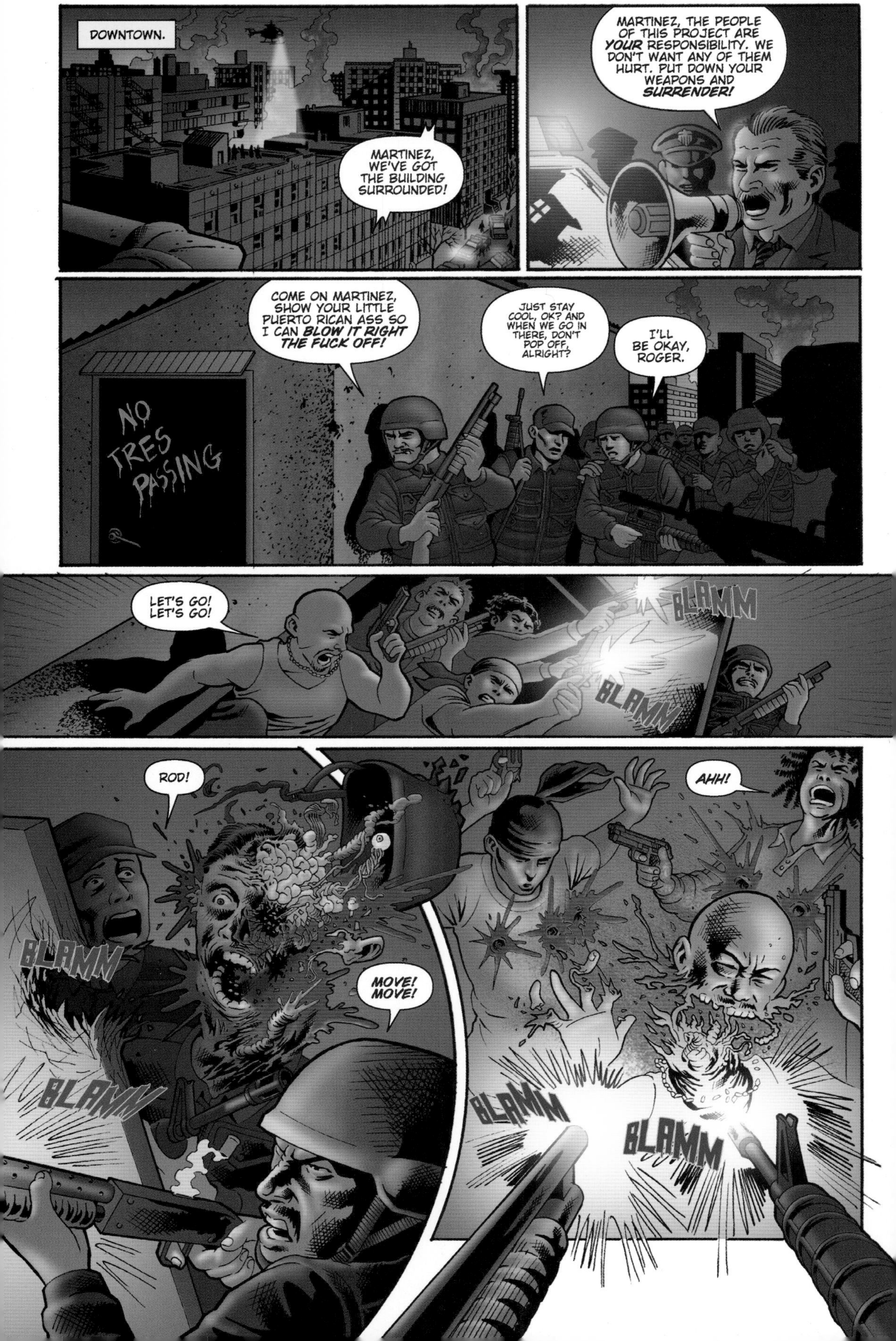
DOWNTOWN.
MARTINEZ, WE'VE GOT THE BUILDING SURROUNDED!
MARTINEZ, THE PEOPLE OF THIS PROJECT ARE YOUR RESPONSIBILITY. WE DON'T WANT ANY OF THEM HURT. PUT DOWN YOUR WEAPONS AND SURRENDER!
COME ON MARTINEZ, SHOW YOUR LITTLE PUERTO RICAN ASS SO I CAN BLOW IT RIGHT THE FUCK OFF!
NO TRES PASSING
JUST STAY COOL, OK? AND WHEN WE GO IN THERE, DON'T POP OFF, ALRIGHT?
I'LL BE OKAY, ROGER.
LET'S GO! LET'S GO!
BLAMM
BLAMM
ROD!
AHH!
BLAMM
MOVE! MOVE!
BLAMM
BLAMM
BLAMM

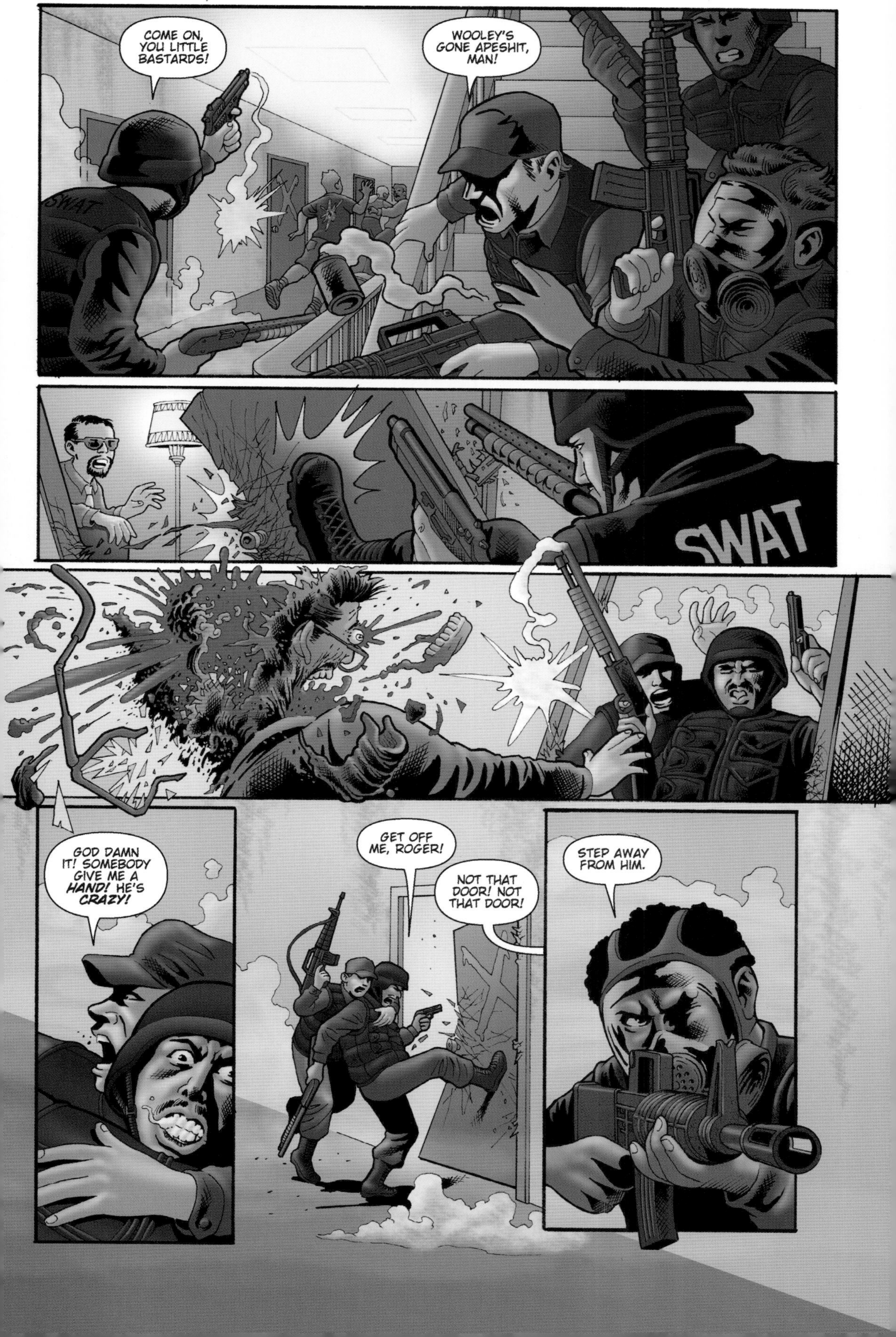
COME ON, YOU LITTLE BASTARDS!
WOOLEY'S GONE APESHIT, MAN!
SWAT
SWAT
GOD DAMN IT! SOMEBODY GIVE ME A *HAND!* HE'S *CRAZY!*
GET OFF ME, ROGER!
NOT THAT DOOR! NOT THAT DOOR!
STEP AWAY FROM HIM.

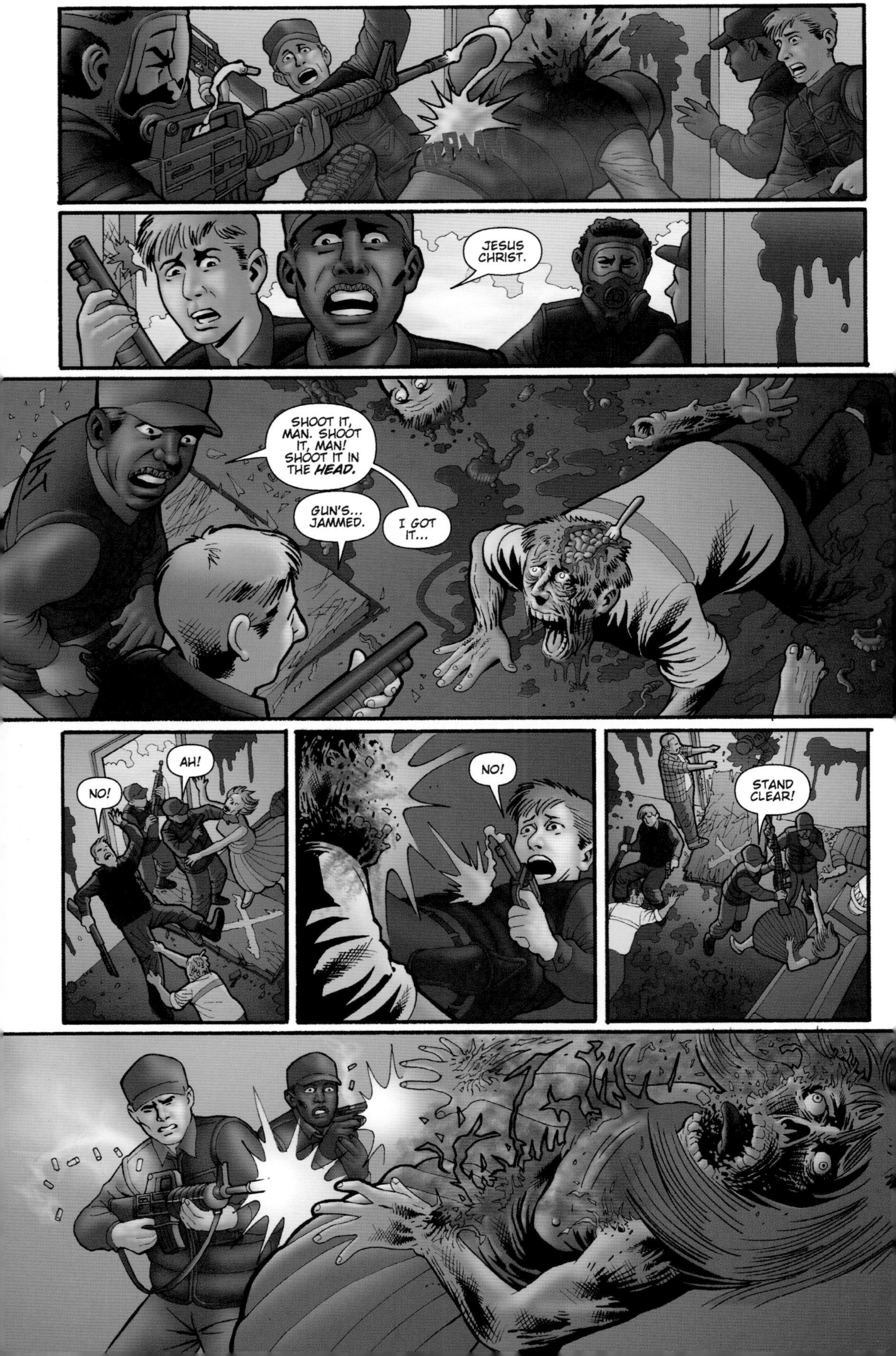
JESUS CHRIST.
SHOOT IT, MAN. SHOOT IT, MAN! SHOOT IT IN THE *HEAD.*
GUN'S... JAMMED.
I GOT IT...
NO!
AH!
NO!
STAND CLEAR!

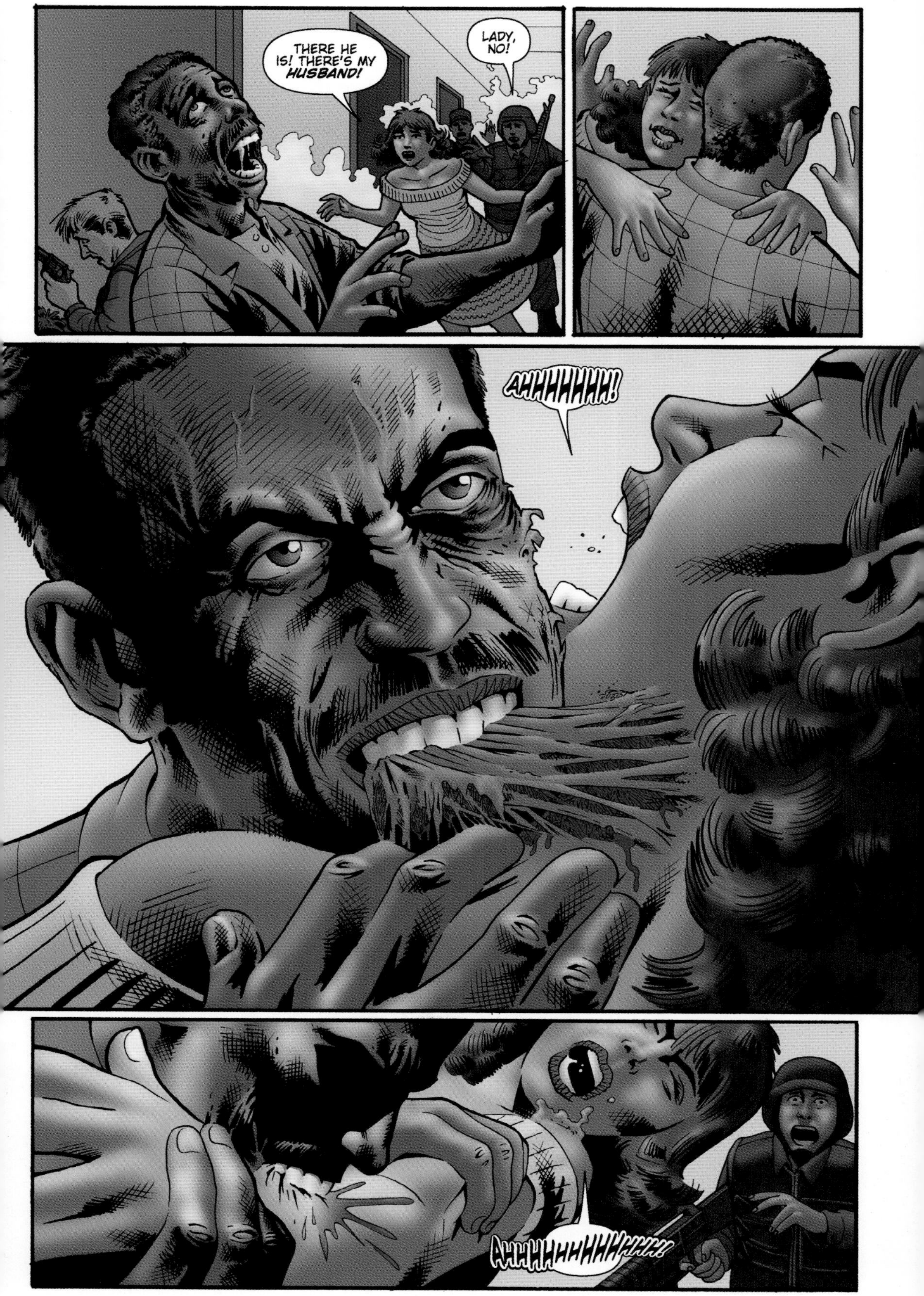
THERE HE IS! THERE'S MY HUSBAND!
LADY, NO!
AHHHHHHH!
AHHHHHHHHHHHH!!

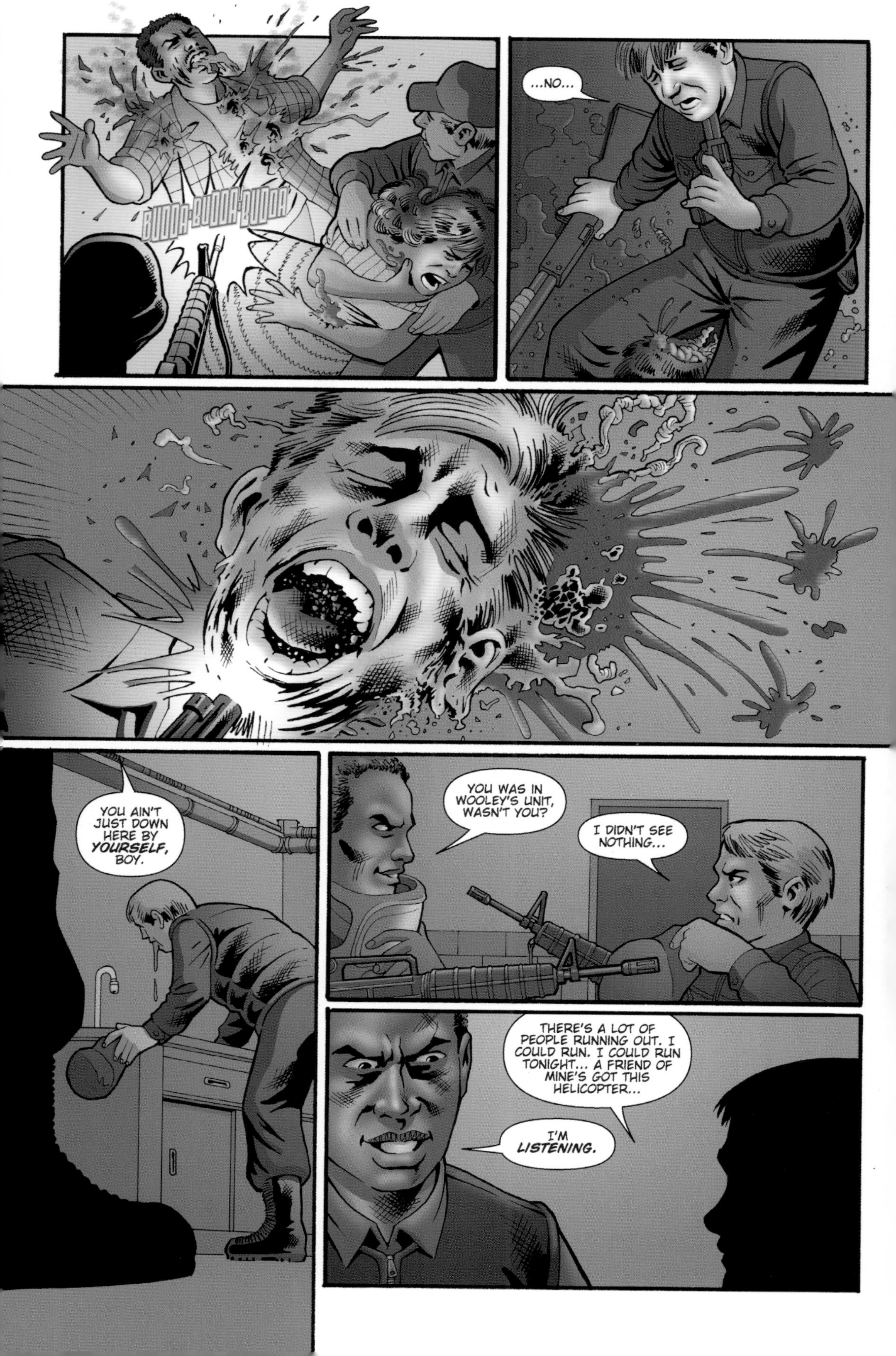
BUDDA BUDDA BUDDA
...NO...
YOU AIN'T JUST DOWN HERE BY YOURSELF, BOY.
YOU WAS IN WOOLEY'S UNIT, WASN'T YOU?
I DIDN'T SEE NOTHING...
THERE'S A LOT OF PEOPLE RUNNING OUT. I COULD RUN. I COULD RUN TONIGHT... A FRIEND OF MINE'S GOT THIS HELICOPTER...
I'M LISTENING.

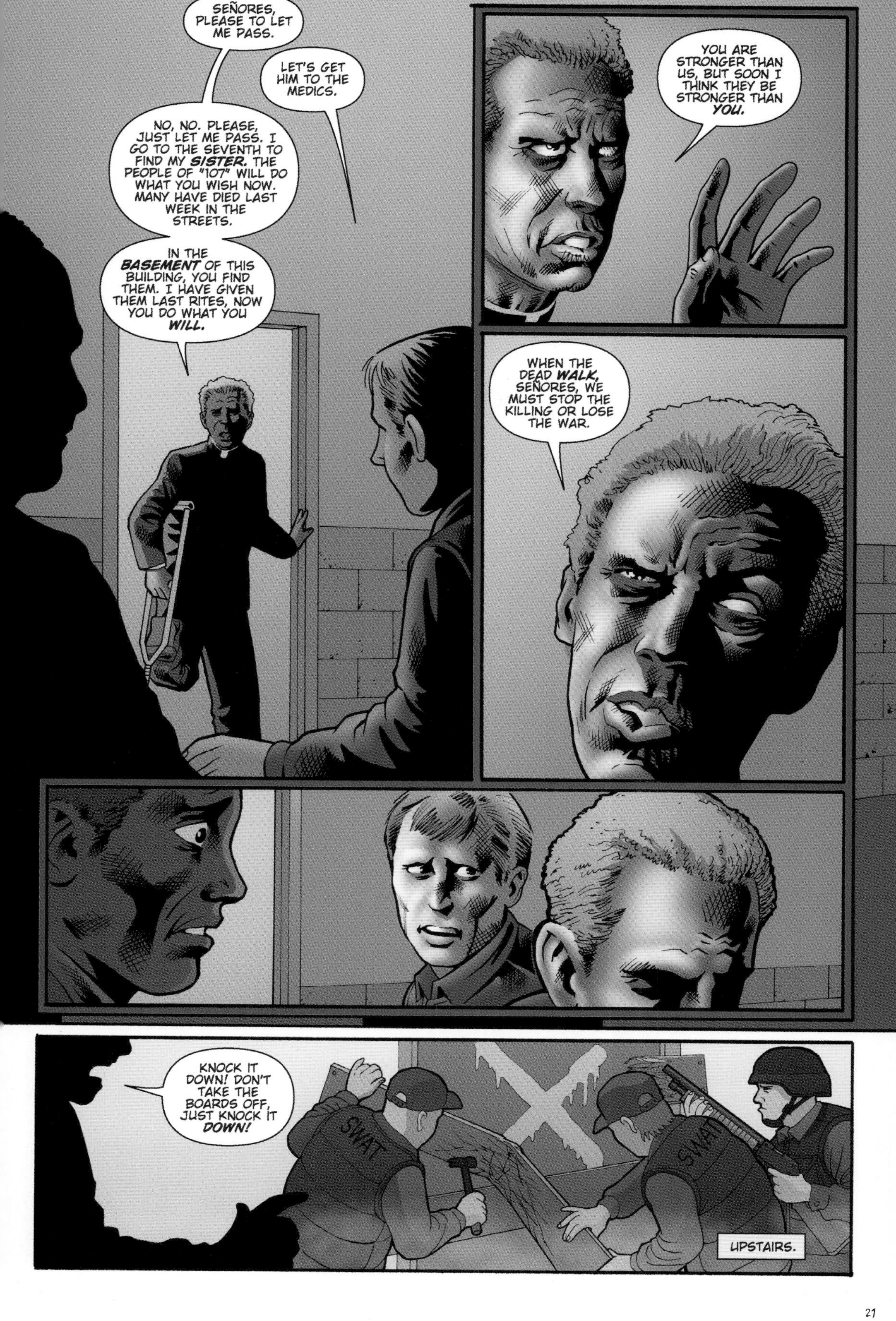
SEÑORES, PLEASE TO LET ME PASS.
LET'S GET HIM TO THE MEDICS.
NO, NO. PLEASE, JUST LET ME PASS. I GO TO THE SEVENTH TO FIND MY SISTER. THE PEOPLE OF "107" WILL DO WHAT YOU WISH NOW. MANY HAVE DIED LAST WEEK IN THE STREETS.
IN THE BASEMENT OF THIS BUILDING, YOU FIND THEM. I HAVE GIVEN THEM LAST RITES, NOW YOU DO WHAT YOU WILL.
YOU ARE STRONGER THAN US, BUT SOON I THINK THEY BE STRONGER THAN YOU.
WHEN THE DEAD WALK, SEÑORES, WE MUST STOP THE KILLING OR LOSE THE WAR.
KNOCK IT DOWN! DON'T TAKE THE BOARDS OFF, JUST KNOCK IT DOWN!
SWAT
SWAT
UPSTAIRS.

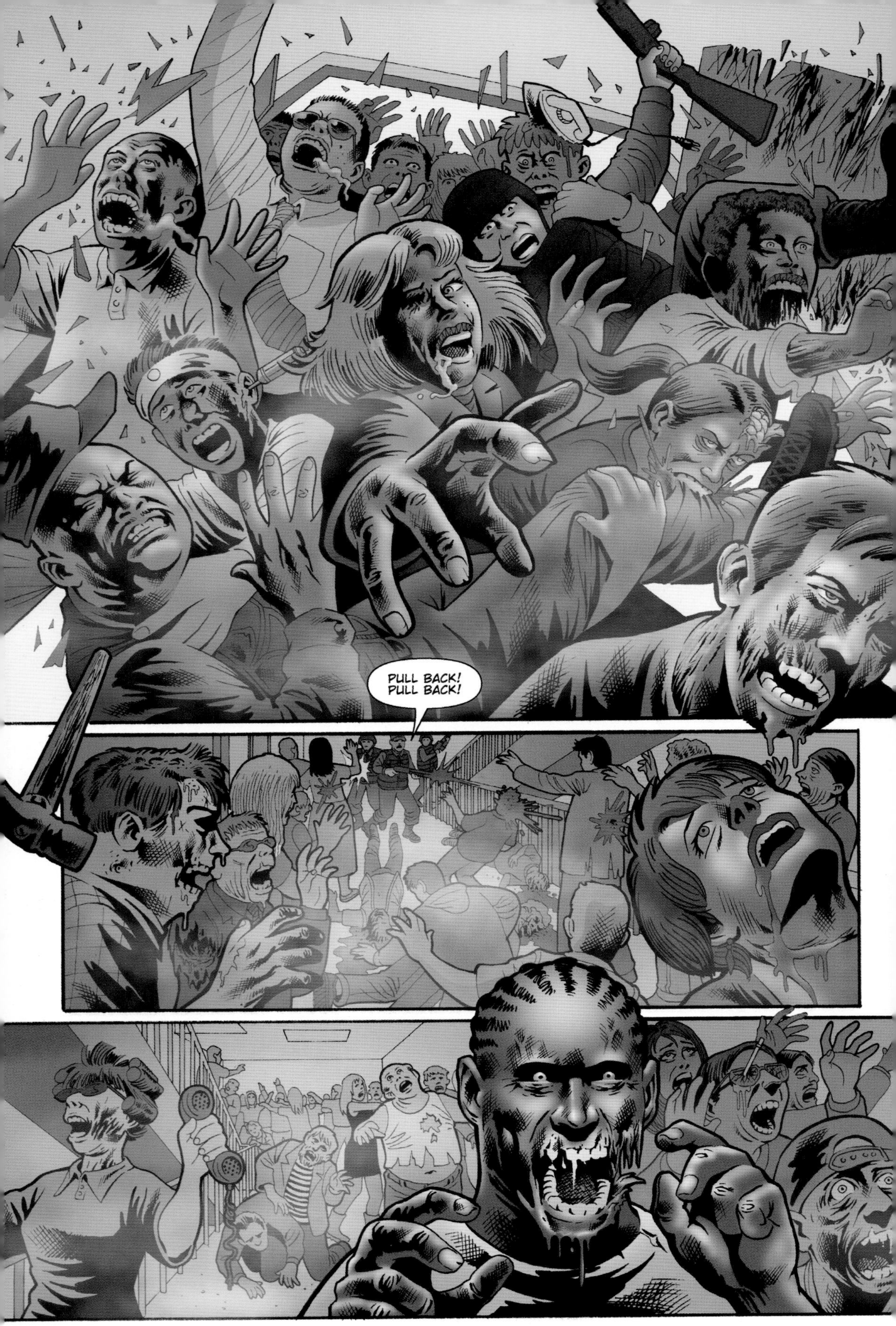
PULL BACK!
PULL BACK!

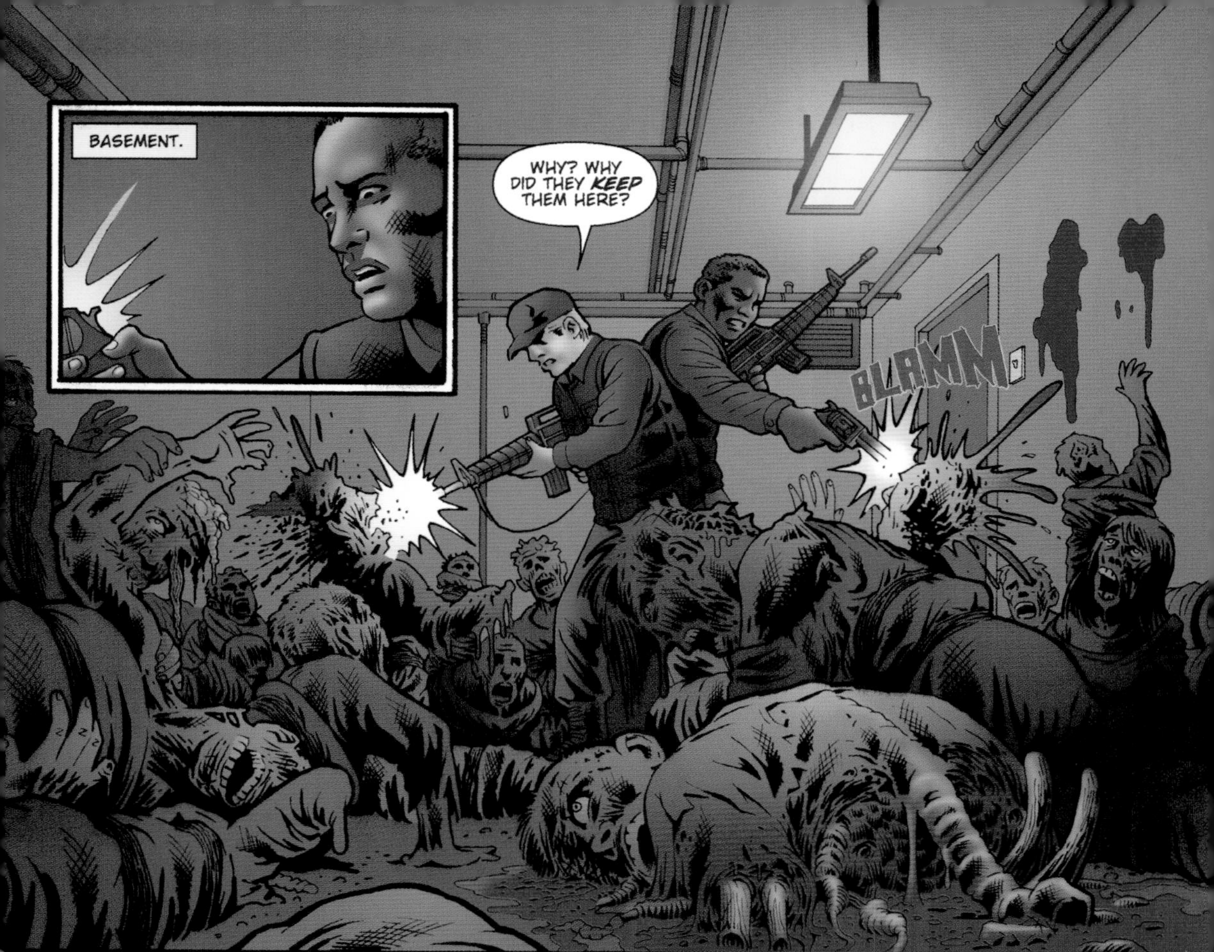
BASEMENT.
WHY? WHY DID THEY KEEP THEM HERE?
BLAMM
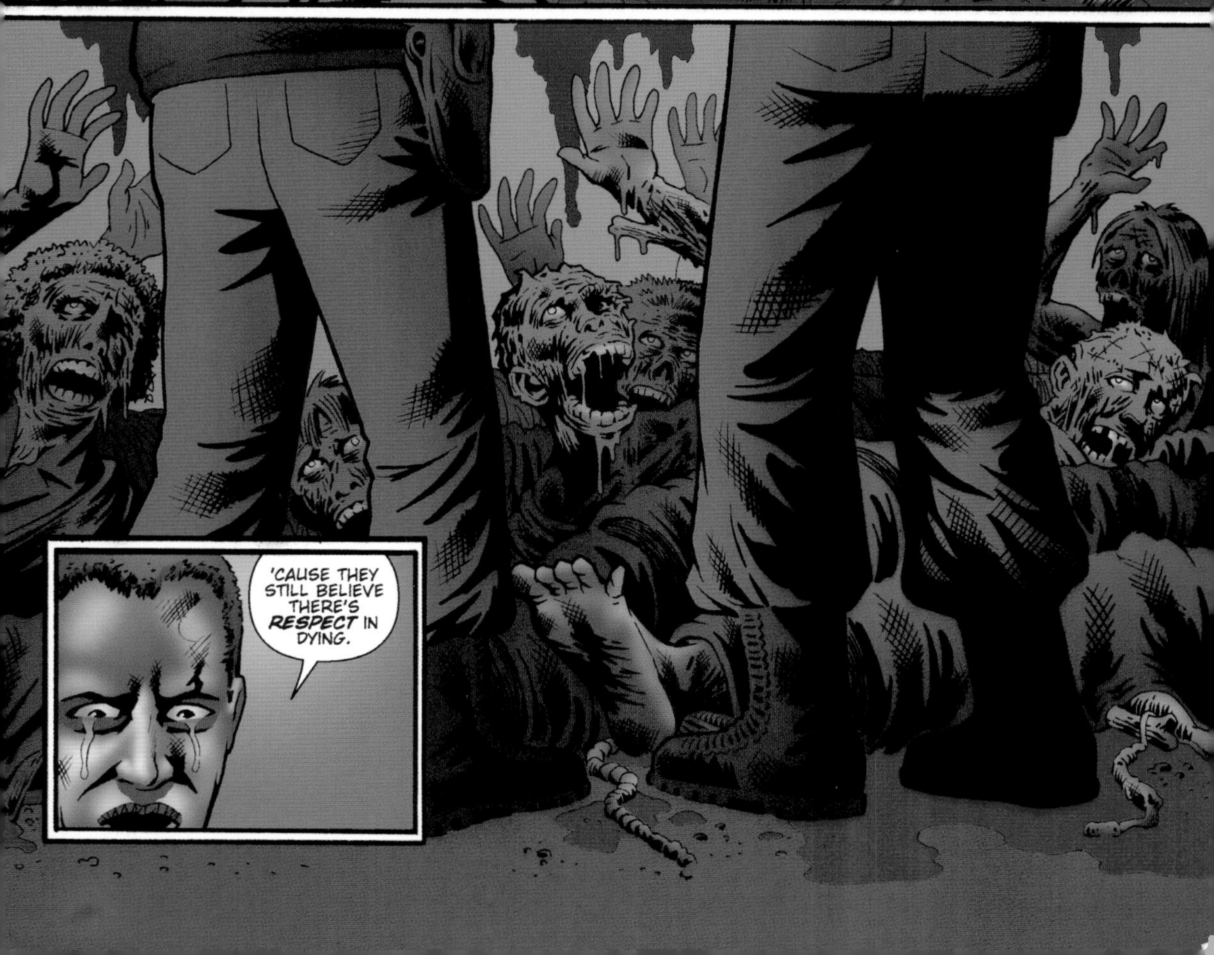
'CAUSE THEY STILL BELIEVE THERE'S RESPECT IN DYING.

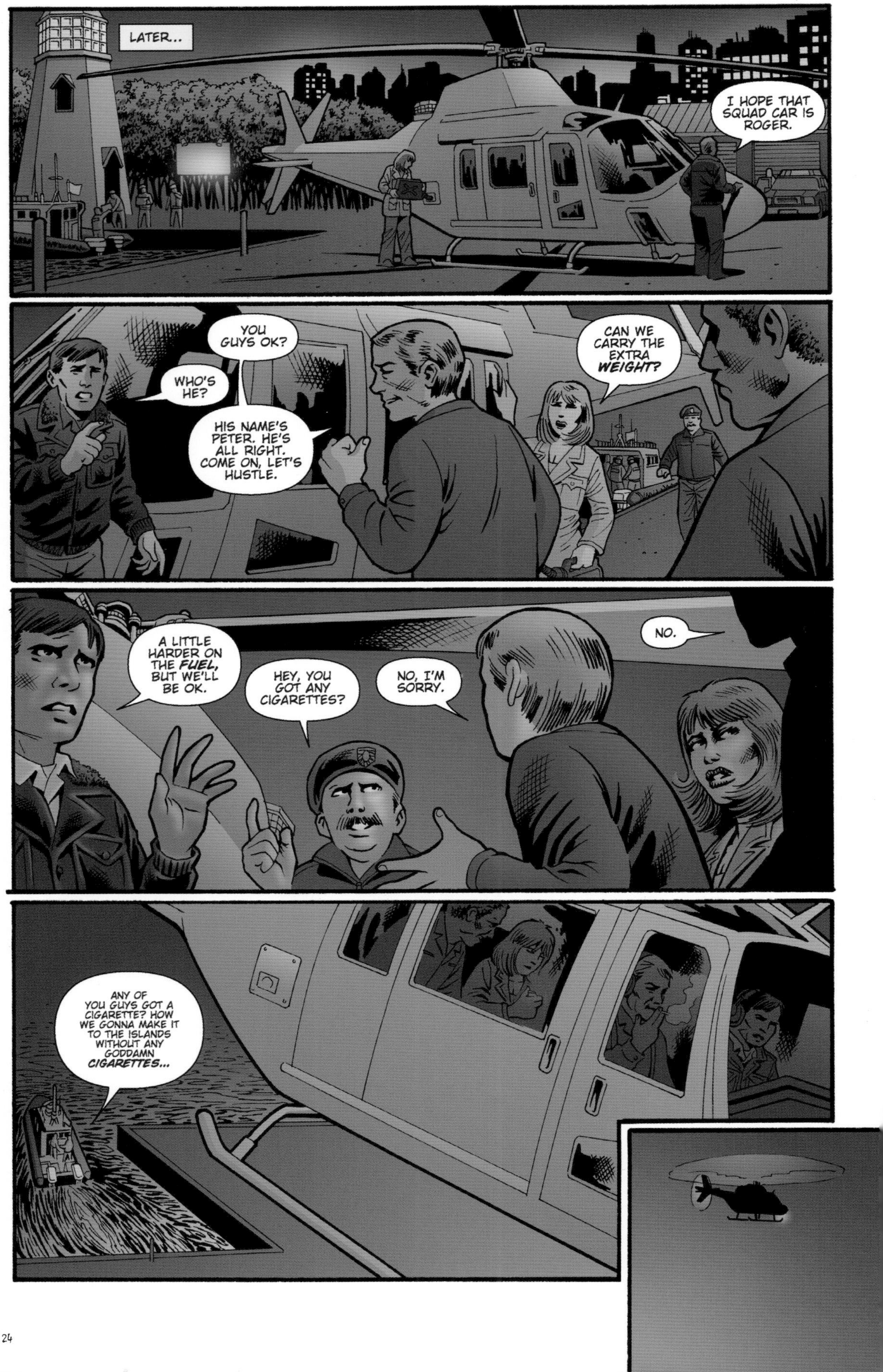
LATER...
I HOPE THAT SQUAD CAR IS ROGER.
WHO'S HE?
YOU GUYS OK?
HIS NAME'S PETER. HE'S ALL RIGHT. COME ON, LET'S HUSTLE.
CAN WE CARRY THE EXTRA *WEIGHT?*
A LITTLE HARDER ON THE *FUEL,* BUT WE'LL BE OK.
HEY, YOU GOT ANY CIGARETTES?
NO, I'M SORRY.
NO.
ANY OF YOU GUYS GOT A CIGARETTE? HOW WE GONNA MAKE IT TO THE ISLANDS WITHOUT ANY GODDAMN *CIGARETTES...*

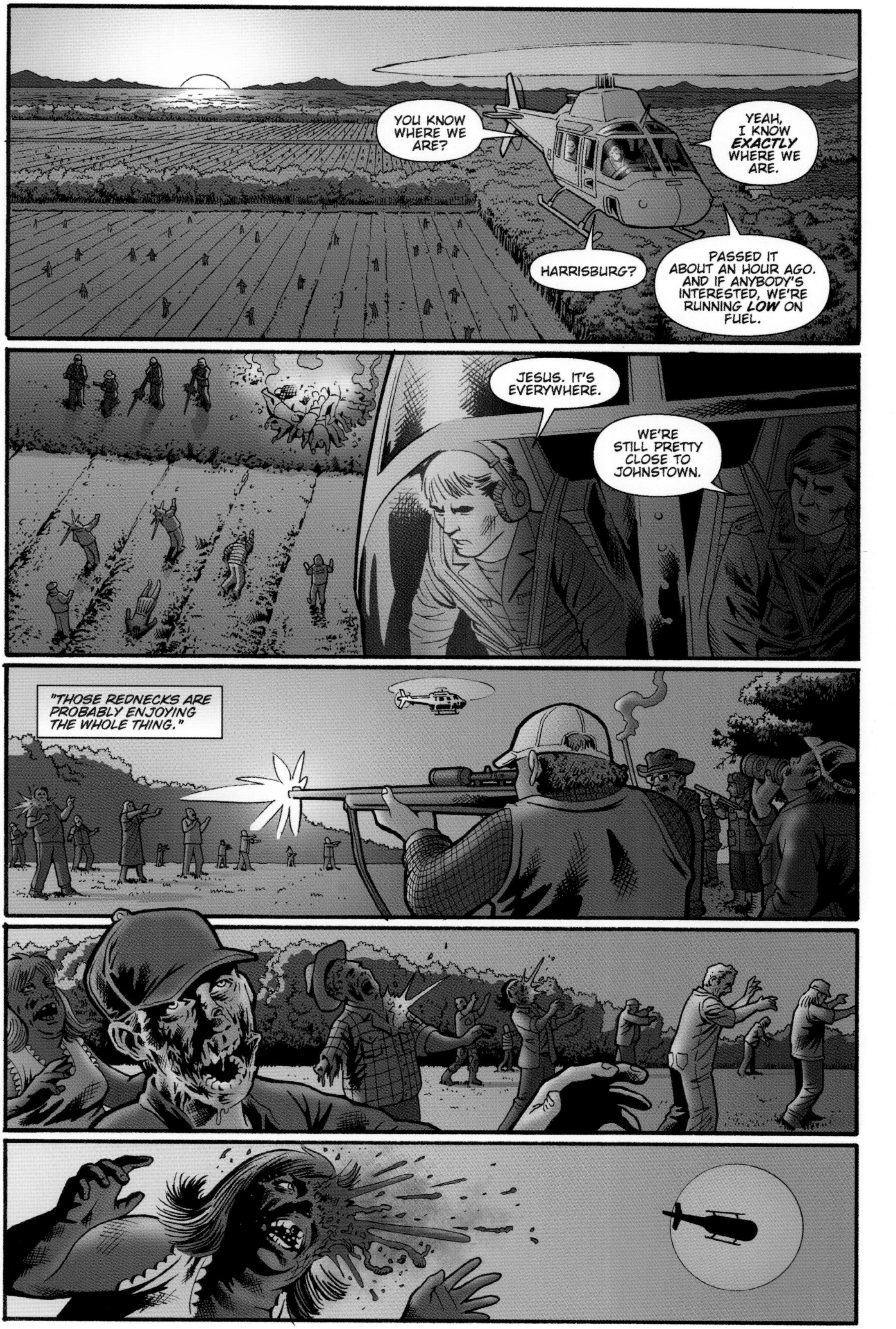
YOU KNOW WHERE WE ARE?
YEAH, I KNOW **EXACTLY** WHERE WE ARE.
HARRISBURG?
PASSED IT ABOUT AN HOUR AGO. AND IF ANYBODY'S INTERESTED, WE'RE RUNNING **LOW** ON FUEL.
JESUS. IT'S EVERYWHERE.
WE'RE STILL PRETTY CLOSE TO JOHNSTOWN.
"THOSE REDNECKS ARE PROBABLY ENJOYING THE WHOLE THING."

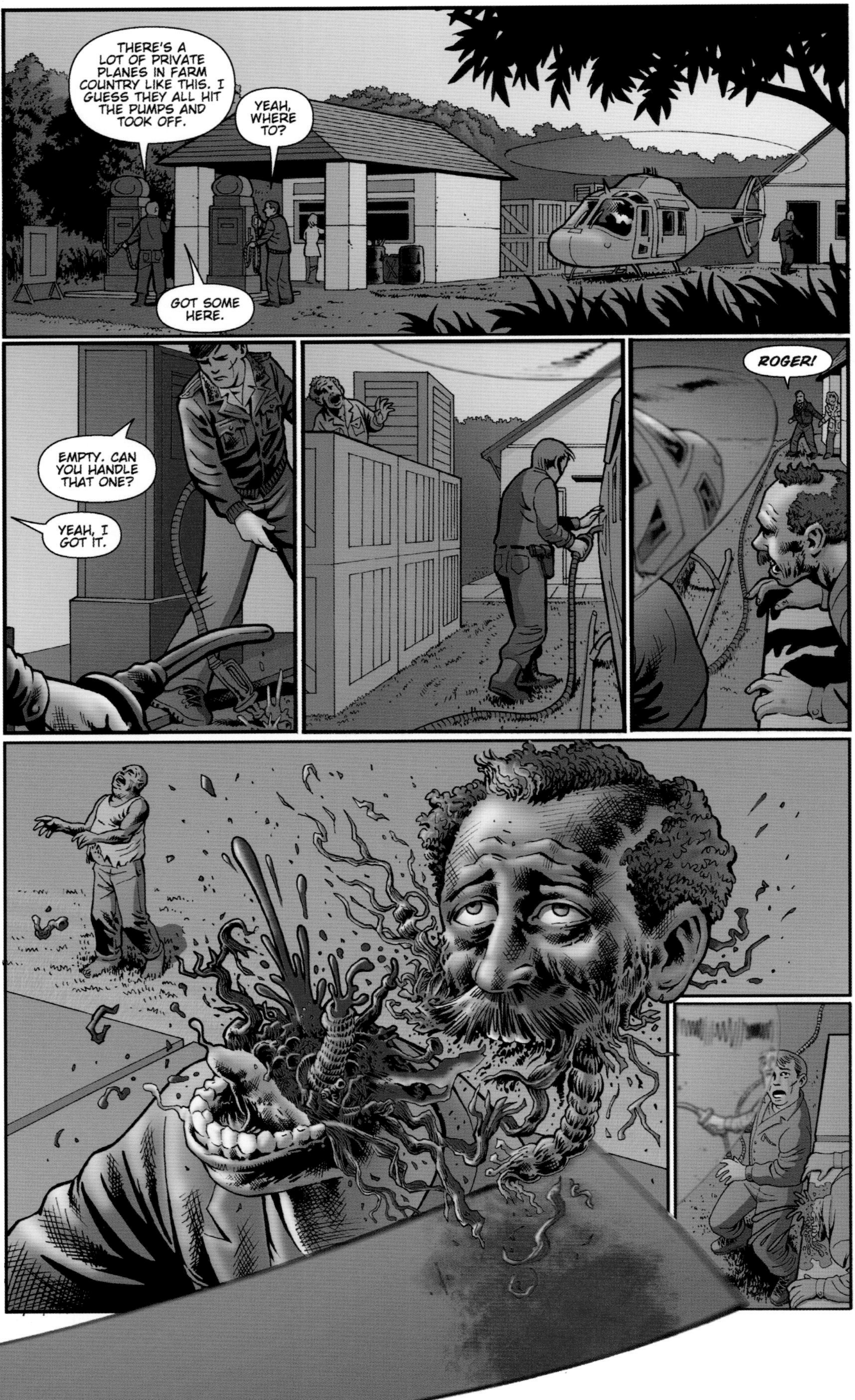
THERE'S A LOT OF PRIVATE PLANES IN FARM COUNTRY LIKE THIS. I GUESS THEY ALL HIT THE PUMPS AND TOOK OFF.
YEAH, WHERE TO?
GOT SOME HERE.
EMPTY. CAN YOU HANDLE THAT ONE?
YEAH, I GOT IT.
ROGER!

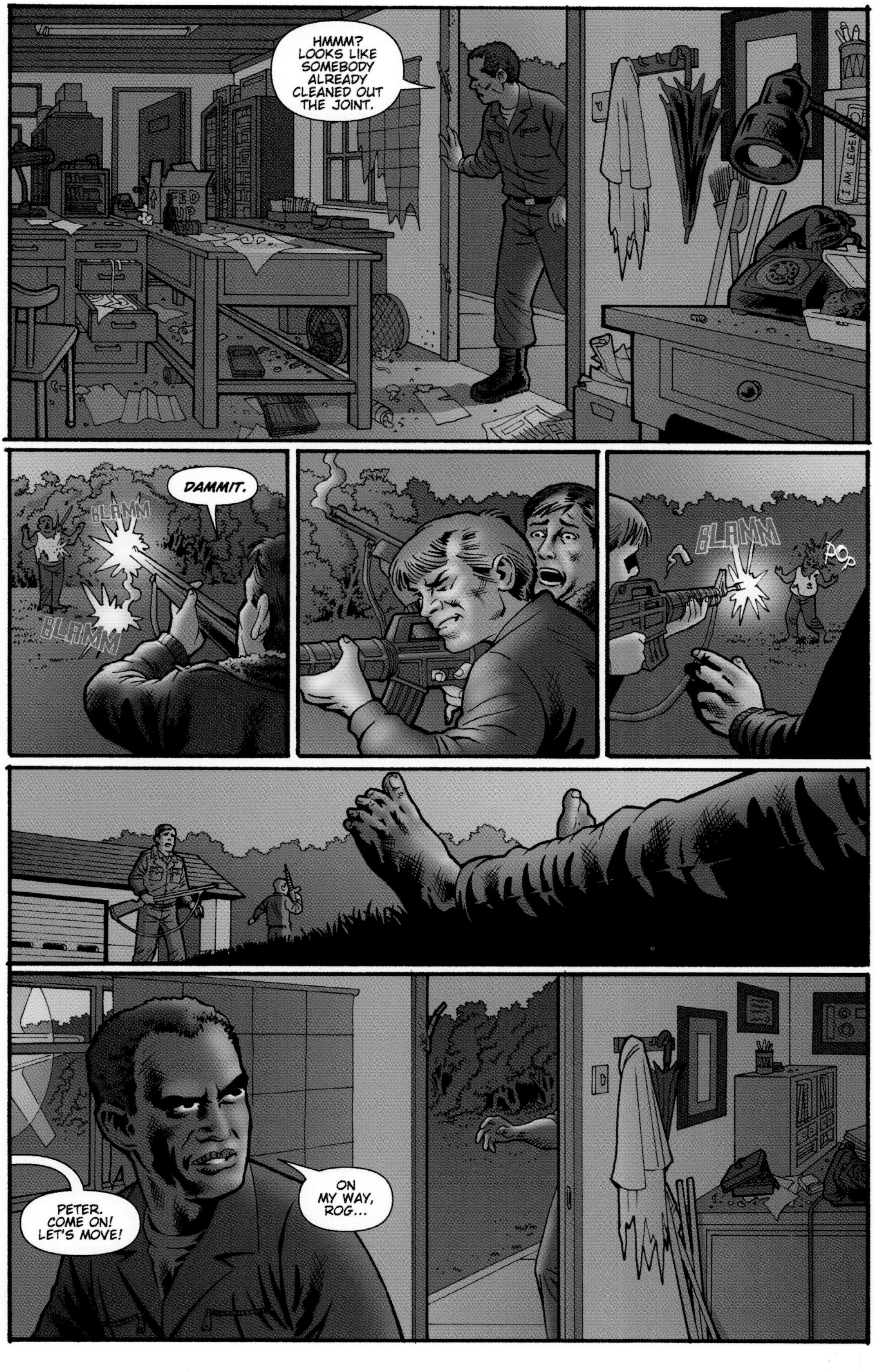
HMMM? LOOKS LIKE SOMEBODY ALREADY CLEANED OUT THE JOINT.
FED UP
I AM LEGEN
DAMMIT.
BLAMM
BLAMM
BLAMM
POP
PETER. COME ON! LET'S MOVE!
ON MY WAY, ROG...

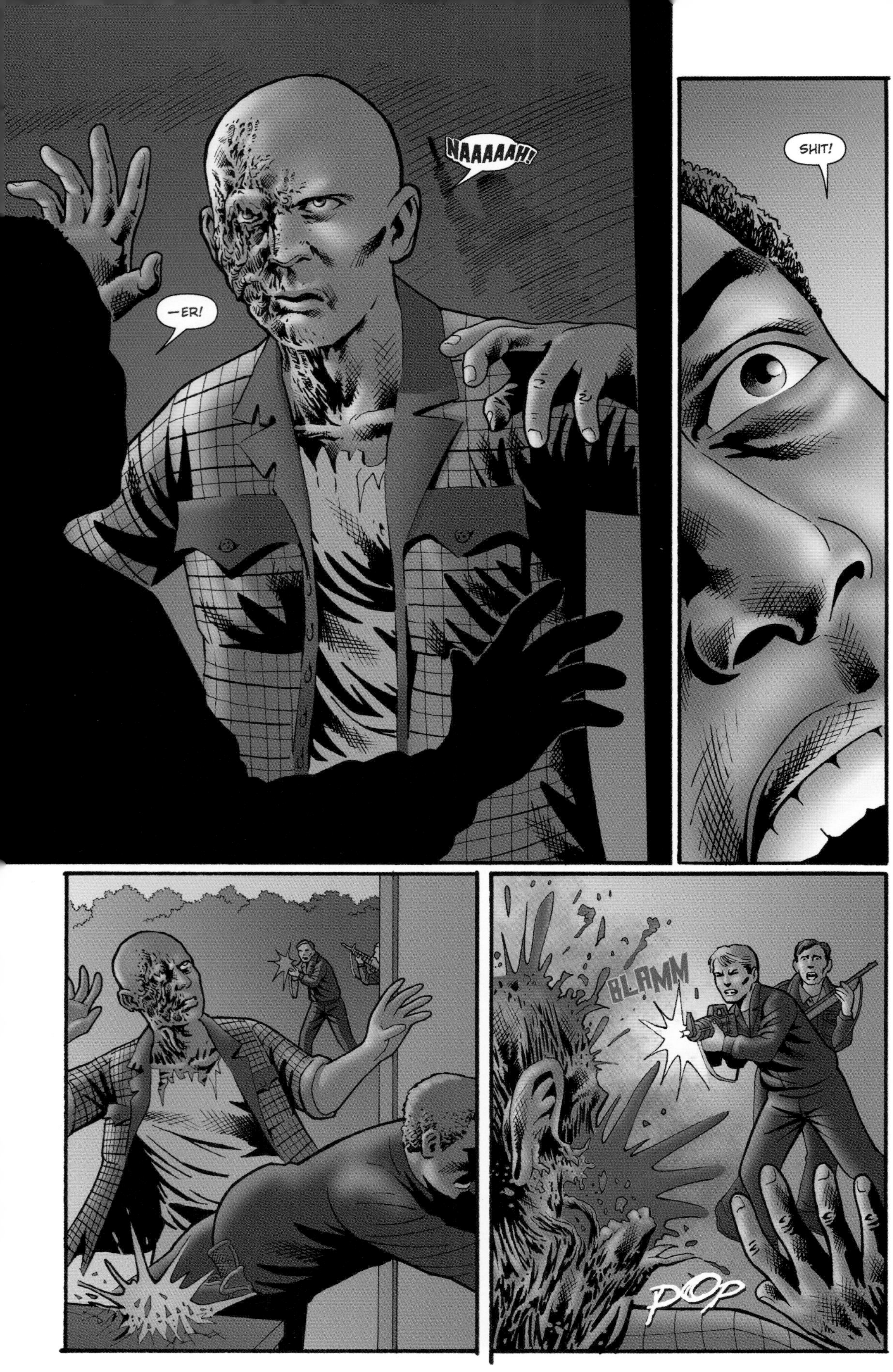
NAAAAAH!
—ER!
SHIT!
BLAMM
POP

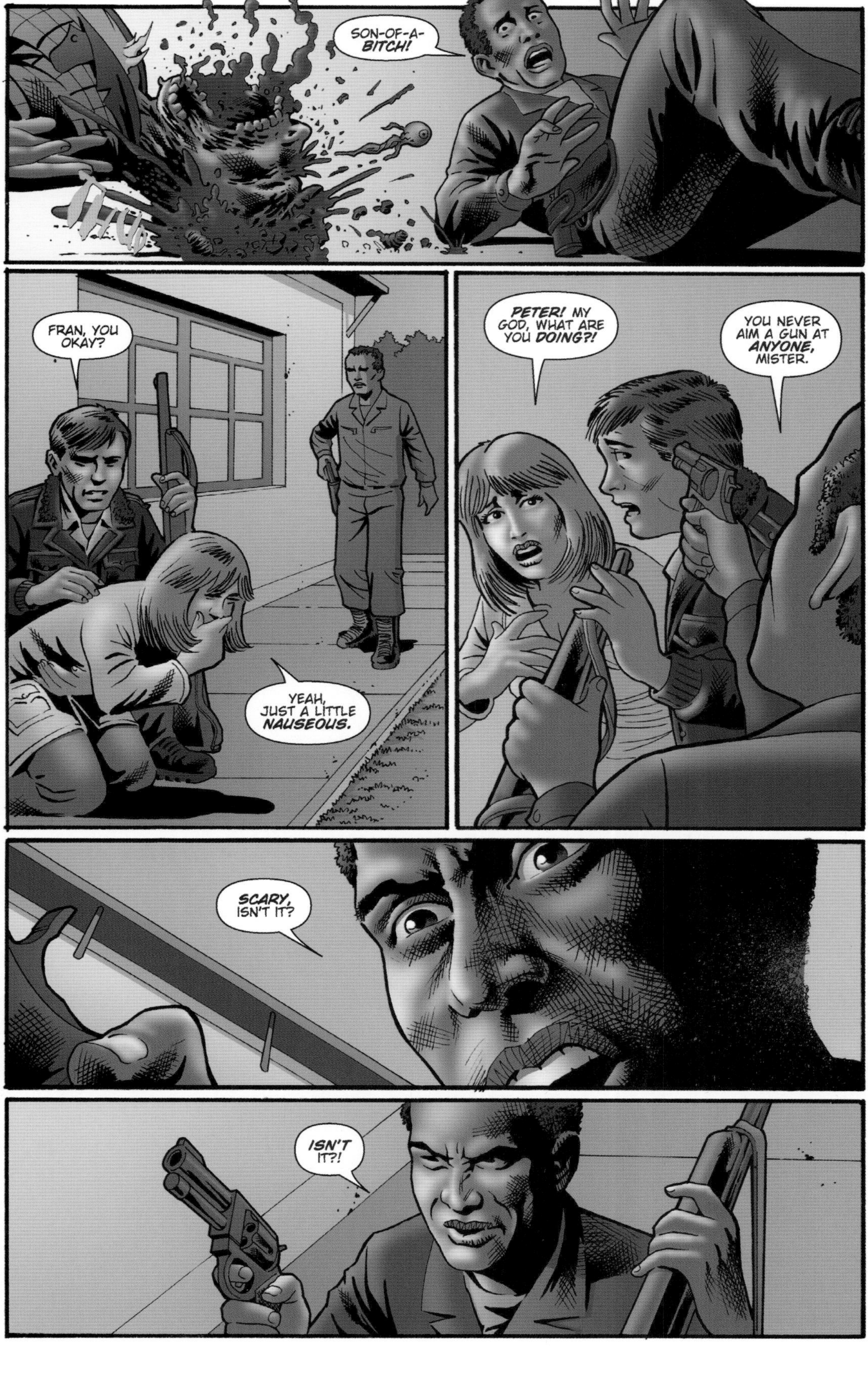
SON-OF-A-BITCH!
FRAN, YOU OKAY?
YEAH, JUST A LITTLE NAUSEOUS.
PETER! MY GOD, WHAT ARE YOU DOING?!
YOU NEVER AIM A GUN AT ANYONE, MISTER.
SCARY, ISN'T IT?
ISN'T IT?!

WE'VE GOT TO FIND FUEL. MAYBE CLOSER TO CLEVELAND.

NO, WE GOT TO STAY *OUT* OF THE BIG CITIES. IF IT'S ANYTHING LIKE PHILLY, WE MAY NEVER GET OUT *ALIVE.*

WE MAY NEVER GET OUT OF ANY PLACE ALIVE. WE ALMOST DIDN'T GET OUT OF *HERE.*

WE'RE GETTING OUT OF HERE FINE, PETER. JUST AS LONG AS THERE AREN'T TOO MANY OF THOSE THINGS AROUND WE CAN HANDLE THEM EASY.

IT WASN'T ONE OF *THOSE* THINGS THAT NEARLY BLEW ME AWAY.

WE'VE GOT TO STAY IN THE STICKS. I MEAN, THERE'S BOUND TO BE MORE LITTLE PRIVATE AIRPORTS UPSTATE.

THERE'S THE LOCKS ALONG THE ALLEGHENY. FUEL STATIONS THERE, STATE AND PRIVATE.

NO, THOSE ARE PROBABLY STILL *MANNED.* WE DON'T NEED THOSE HASSLES EITHER.

THEY'RE JUST OUT AFTER SCAVENGERS AND LOOTERS.

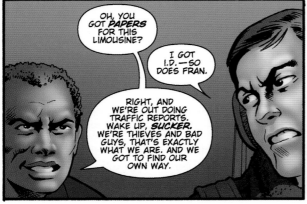

OH, YOU GOT *PAPERS* FOR THIS LIMOUSINE?

I GOT I.D. — SO DOES FRAN.

RIGHT, AND WE'RE OUT DOING TRAFFIC REPORTS. WAKE UP, *SUCKER.* WE'RE THIEVES AND BAD GUYS, THAT'S EXACTLY WHAT WE ARE. AND WE GOT TO FIND OUR OWN WAY.

JESUS CHRIST. WE DON'T EVEN KNOW WHERE WE'RE *GOING.* WE DON'T HAVE FOOD, WE DON'T HAVE WATER, WE DON'T EVEN HAVE A *RADIO!* STEVEN, YOU NEED TO GET SOME SLEEP.

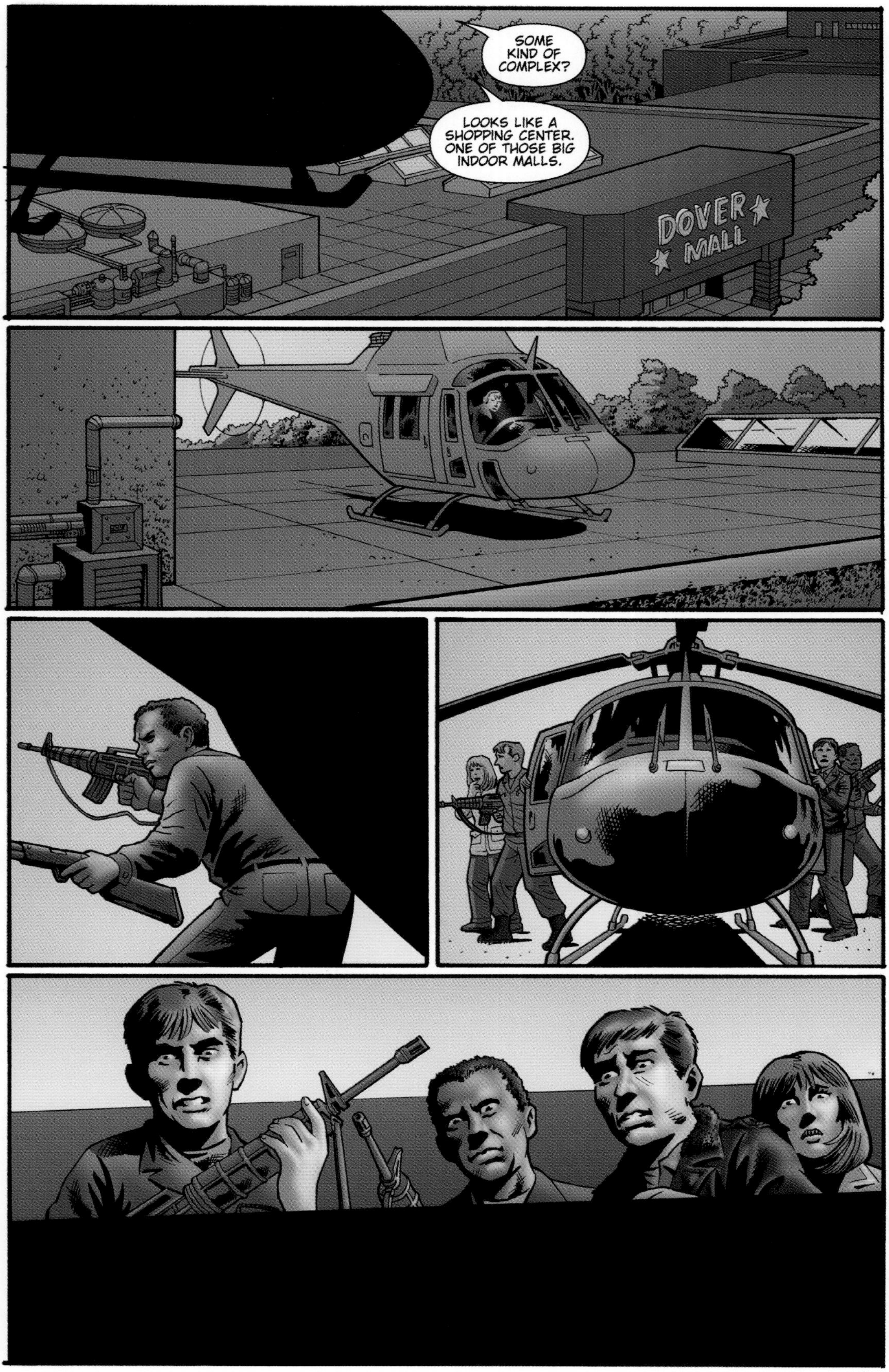
SOME KIND OF COMPLEX?
LOOKS LIKE A SHOPPING CENTER. ONE OF THOSE BIG INDOOR MALLS.
DOVER MALL

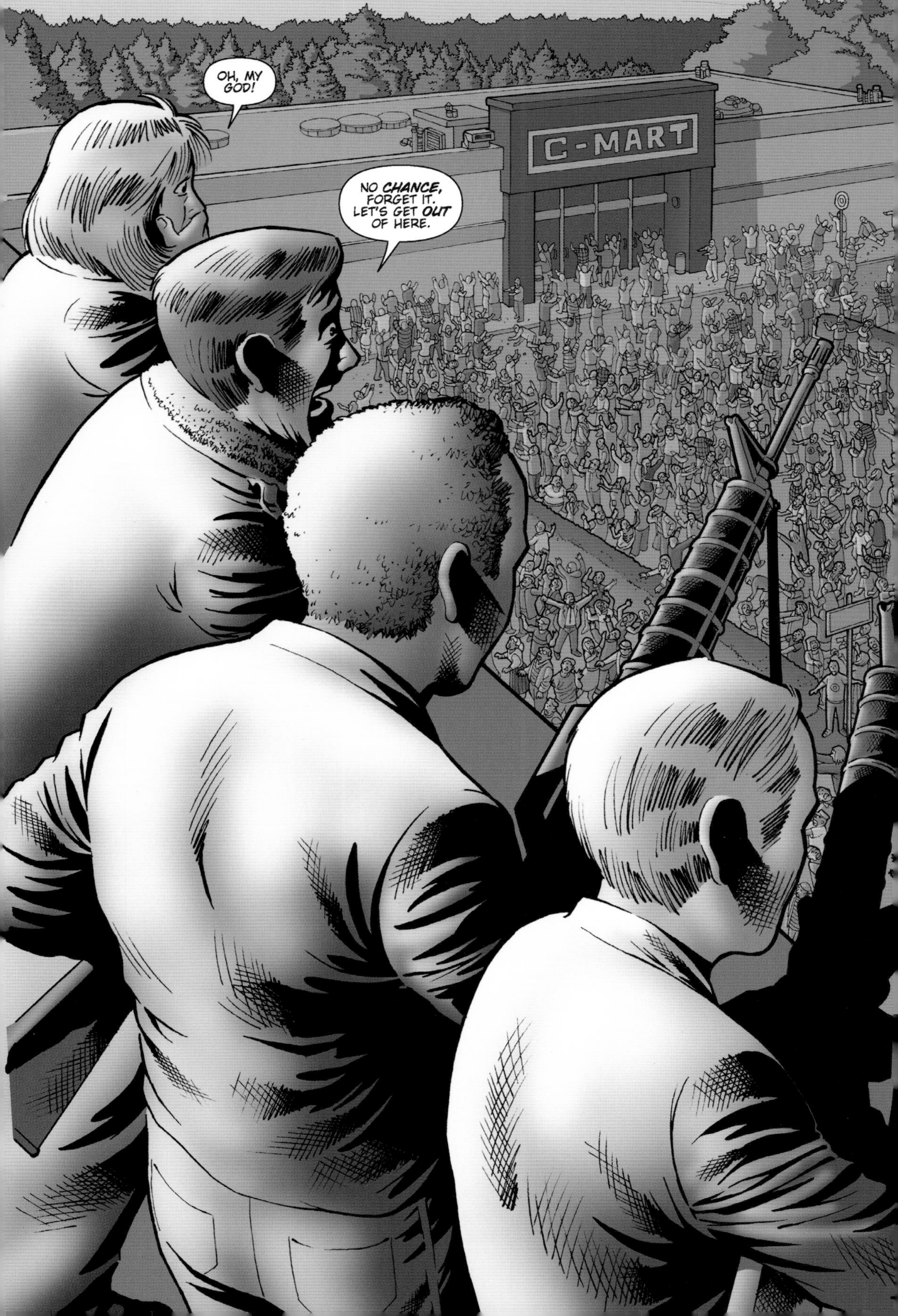
OH, MY GOD!
C-MART
NO CHANCE, FORGET IT. LET'S GET OUT OF HERE.

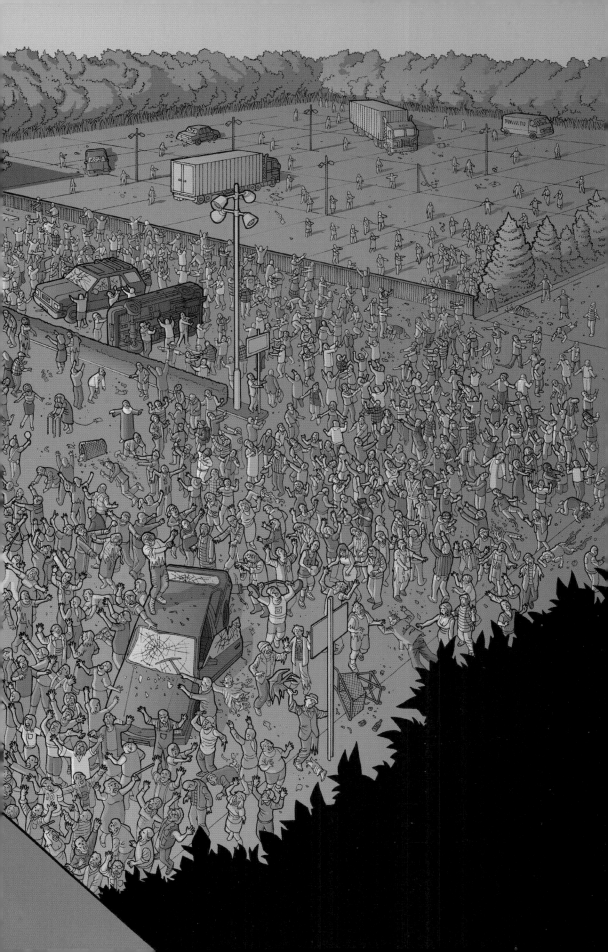

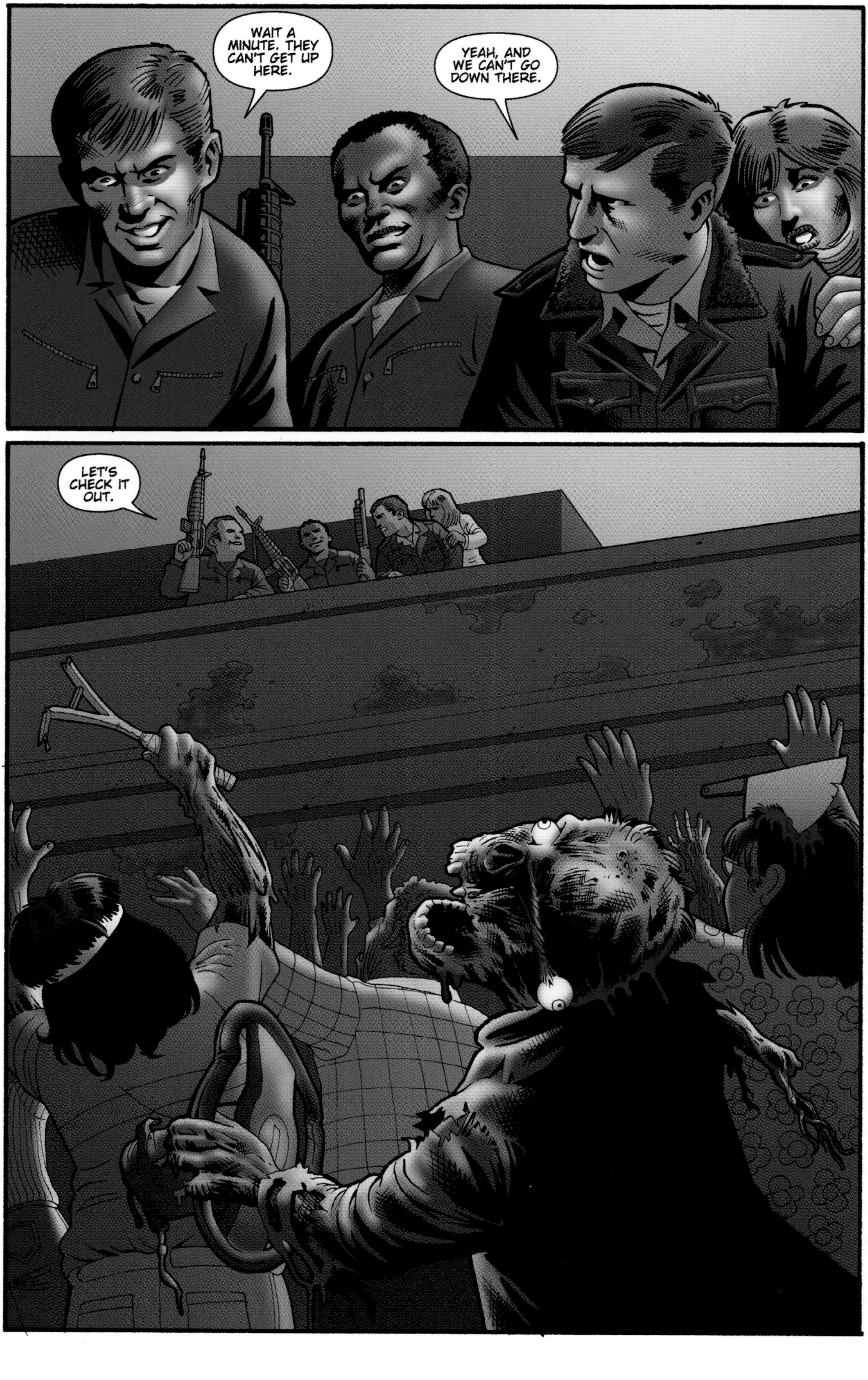
WAIT A MINUTE. THEY CAN'T GET UP HERE.
YEAH, AND WE CAN'T GO DOWN THERE.
LET'S CHECK IT OUT.

Original cover of *Dawn of the Dead* issue 2

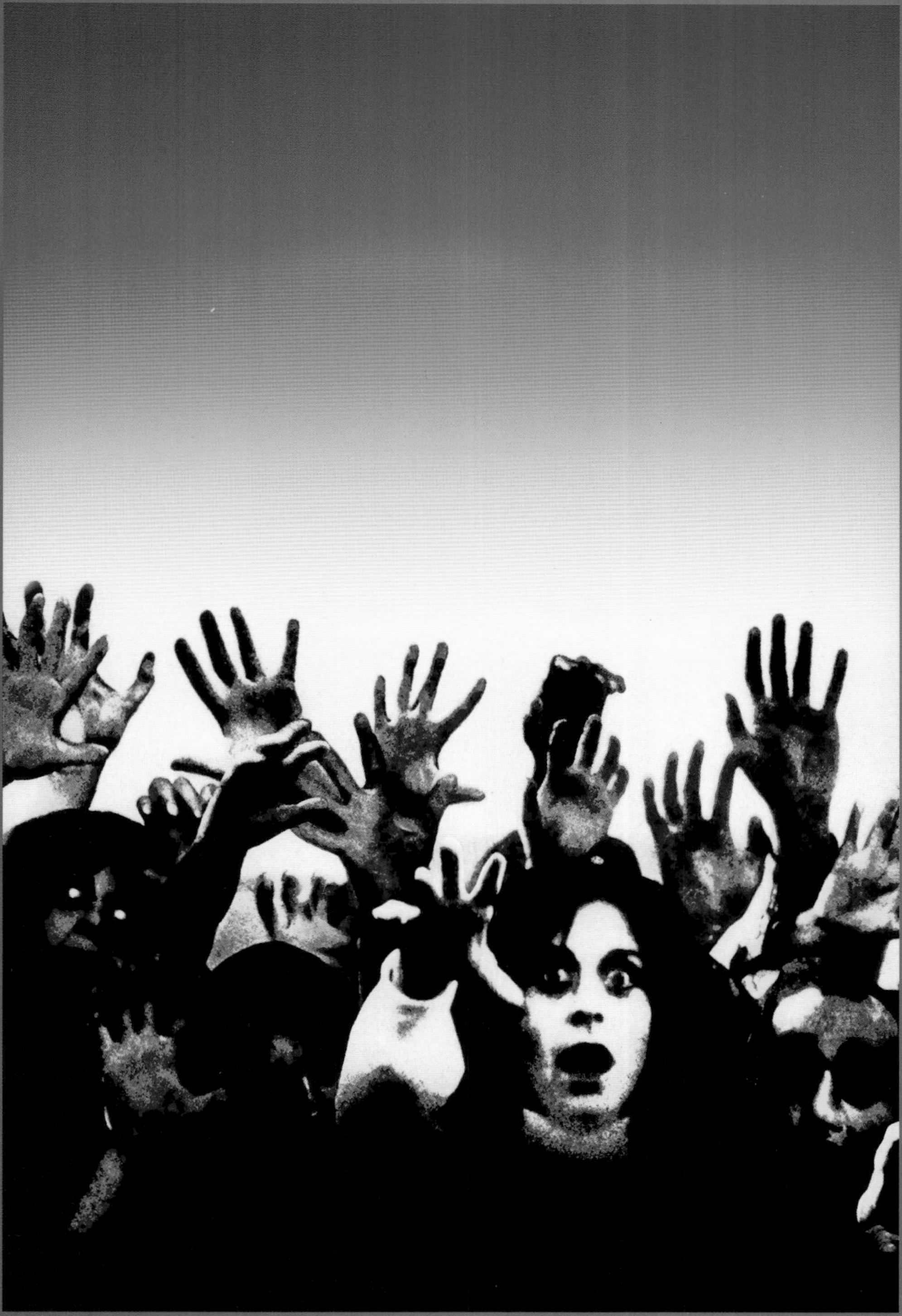

Dawn of the Dead

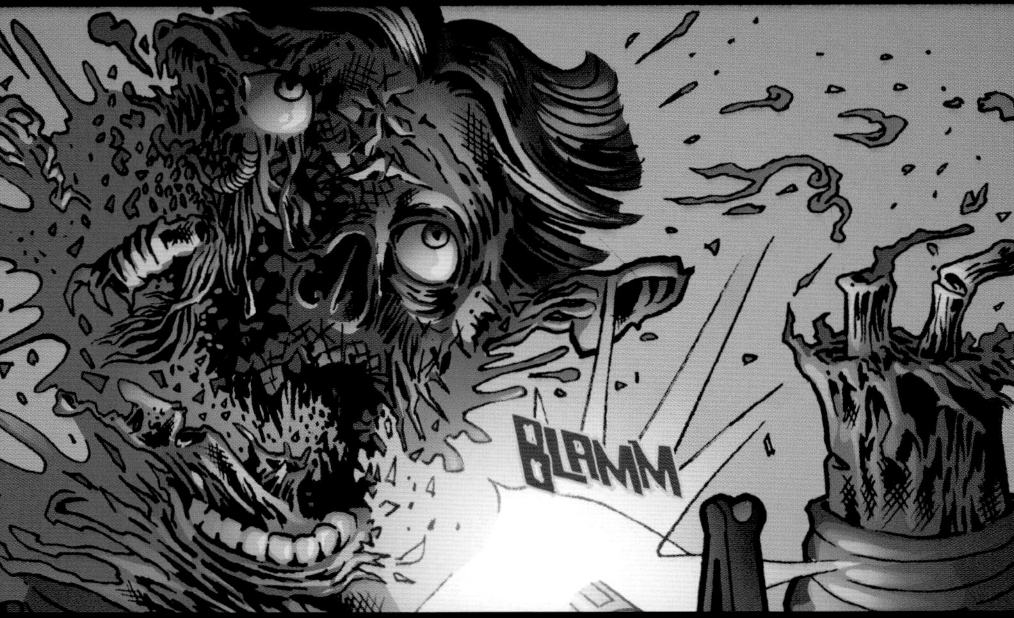
BLAMM

Chapter
-2-

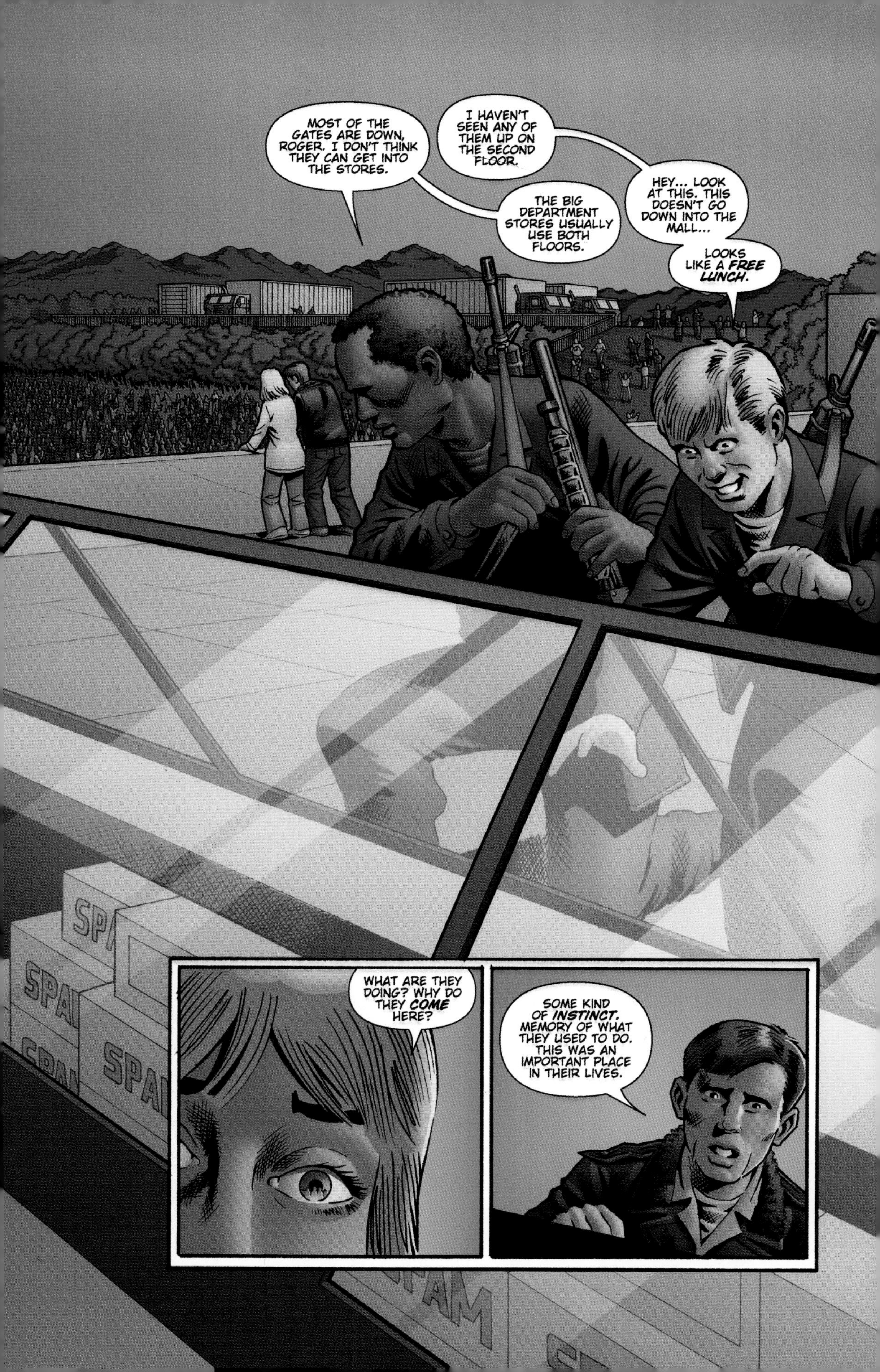
MOST OF THE GATES ARE DOWN, ROGER. I DON'T THINK THEY CAN GET INTO THE STORES.
I HAVEN'T SEEN ANY OF THEM UP ON THE SECOND FLOOR.
THE BIG DEPARTMENT STORES USUALLY USE BOTH FLOORS.
HEY... LOOK AT THIS. THIS DOESN'T GO DOWN INTO THE MALL...
LOOKS LIKE A *FREE LUNCH*.
SPAM
WHAT ARE THEY DOING? WHY DO THEY *COME* HERE?
SOME KIND OF *INSTINCT*. MEMORY OF WHAT THEY USED TO DO. THIS WAS AN IMPORTANT PLACE IN THEIR LIVES.

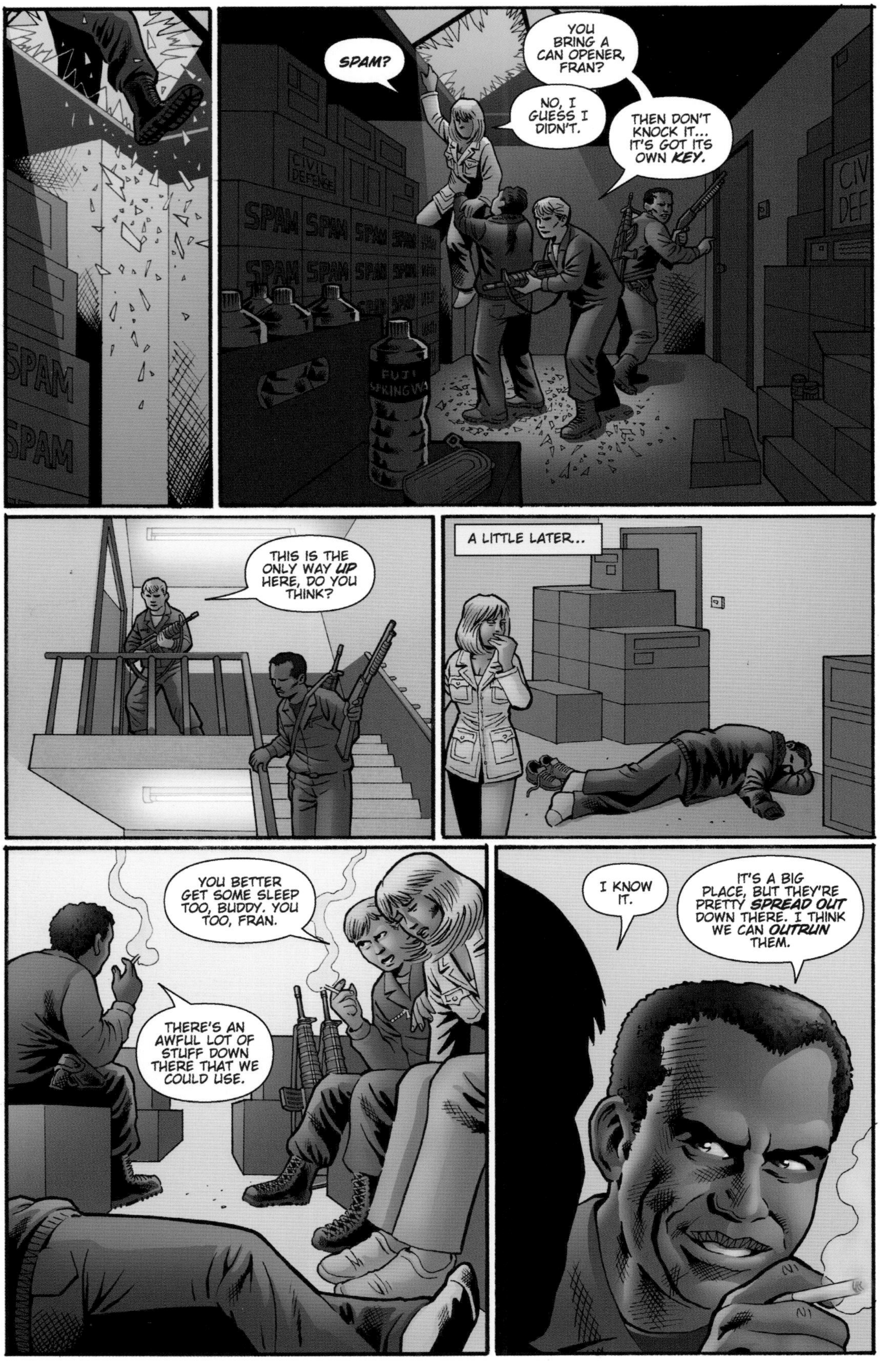
SPAM?
YOU BRING A CAN OPENER, FRAN?
NO, I GUESS I DIDN'T.
THEN DON'T KNOCK IT... IT'S GOT ITS OWN KEY.
CIVIL DEFENSE
SPAM
FUJI SPRINGWA
THIS IS THE ONLY WAY UP HERE, DO YOU THINK?
A LITTLE LATER...
YOU BETTER GET SOME SLEEP TOO, BUDDY. YOU TOO, FRAN.
THERE'S AN AWFUL LOT OF STUFF DOWN THERE THAT WE COULD USE.
I KNOW IT.
IT'S A BIG PLACE, BUT THEY'RE PRETTY SPREAD OUT DOWN THERE. I THINK WE CAN OUTRUN THEM.

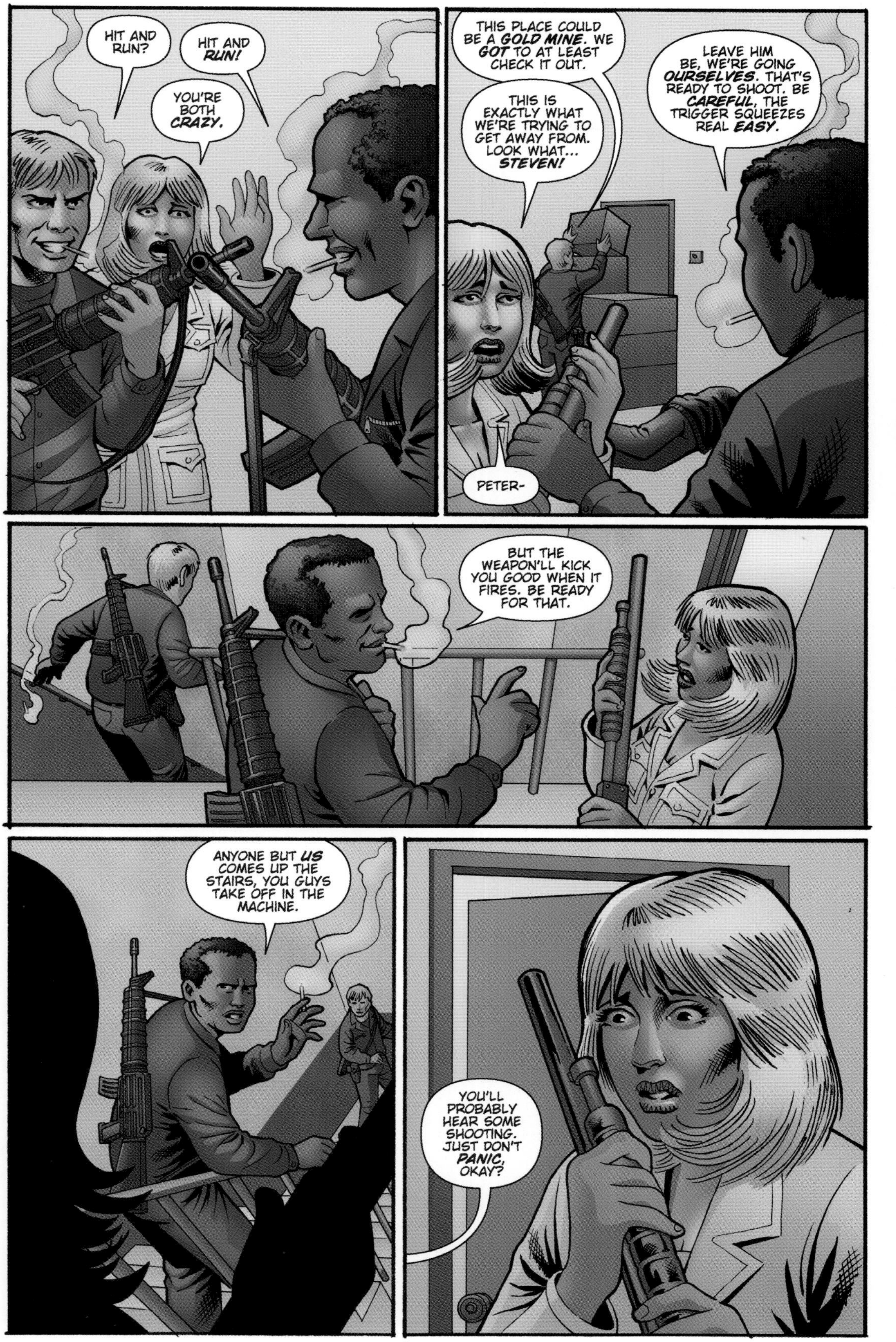

HIT AND RUN?
HIT AND RUN!
YOU'RE BOTH CRAZY.
THIS PLACE COULD BE A GOLD MINE. WE GOT TO AT LEAST CHECK IT OUT.
THIS IS EXACTLY WHAT WE'RE TRYING TO GET AWAY FROM. LOOK WHAT... STEVEN!
LEAVE HIM BE, WE'RE GOING OURSELVES. THAT'S READY TO SHOOT. BE CAREFUL, THE TRIGGER SQUEEZES REAL EASY.
PETER-
BUT THE WEAPON'LL KICK YOU GOOD WHEN IT FIRES. BE READY FOR THAT.
ANYONE BUT US COMES UP THE STAIRS, YOU GUYS TAKE OFF IN THE MACHINE.
YOU'LL PROBABLY HEAR SOME SHOOTING. JUST DON'T PANIC, OKAY?

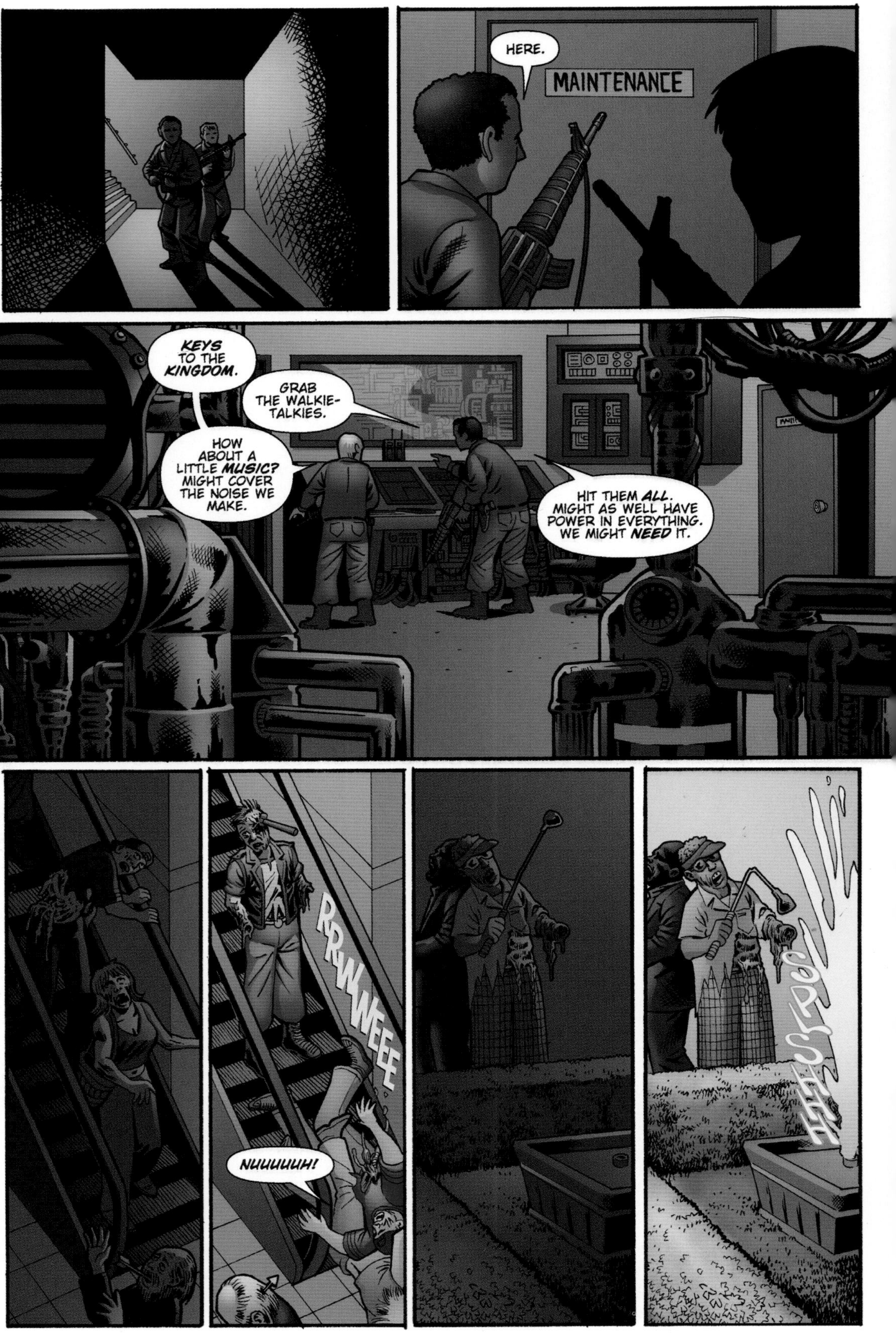
HERE.
MAINTENANCE
KEYS TO THE KINGDOM.
GRAB THE WALKIE-TALKIES.
HOW ABOUT A LITTLE MUSIC? MIGHT COVER THE NOISE WE MAKE.
HIT THEM ALL. MIGHT AS WELL HAVE POWER IN EVERYTHING. WE MIGHT NEED IT.
RRWWEEEE
NUUUUUH!

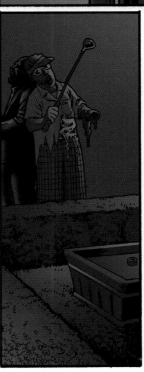

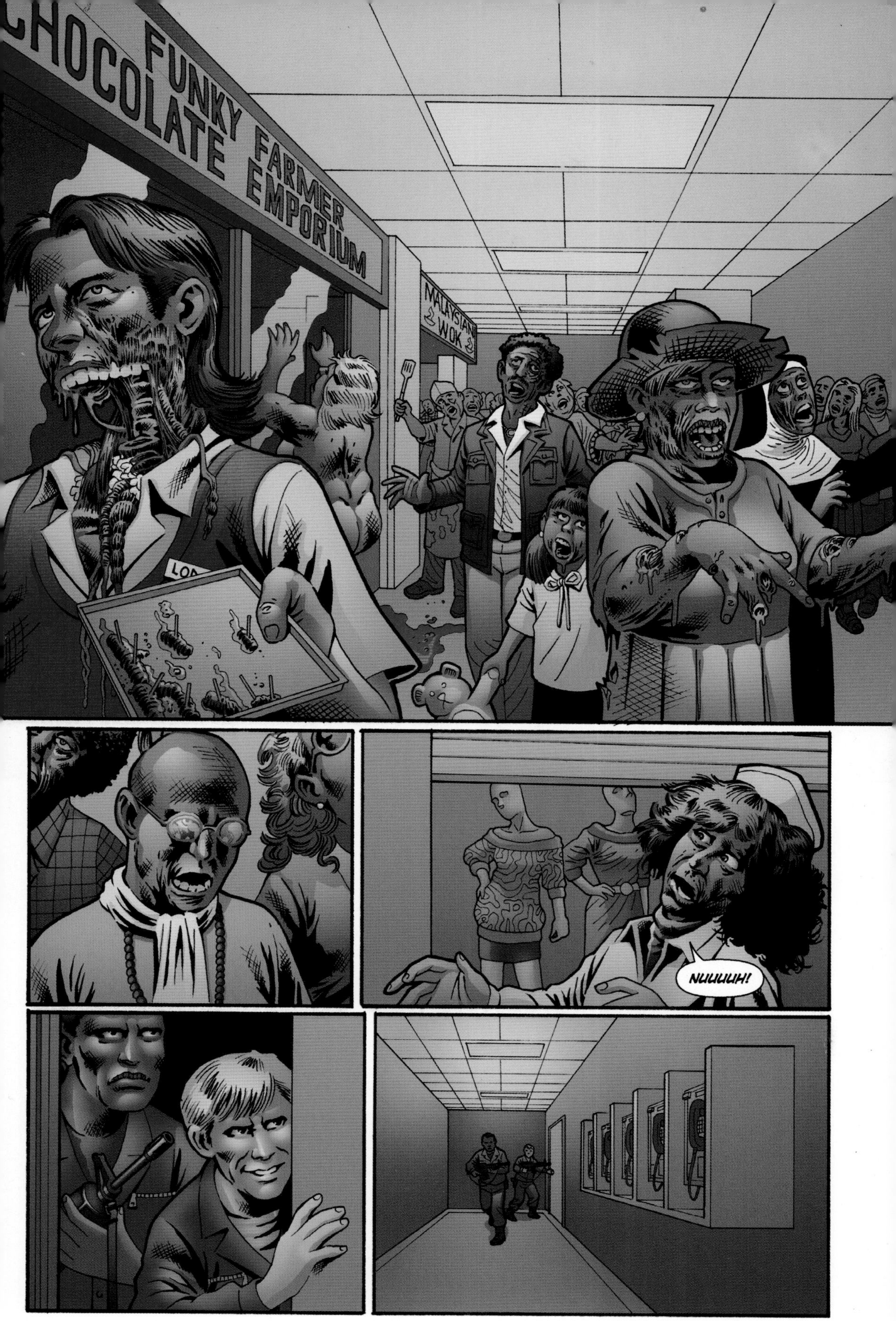
FUNKY FARMER
CHOCOLATE EMPORIUM
MALAYSIAN WOK
NUUUUH!

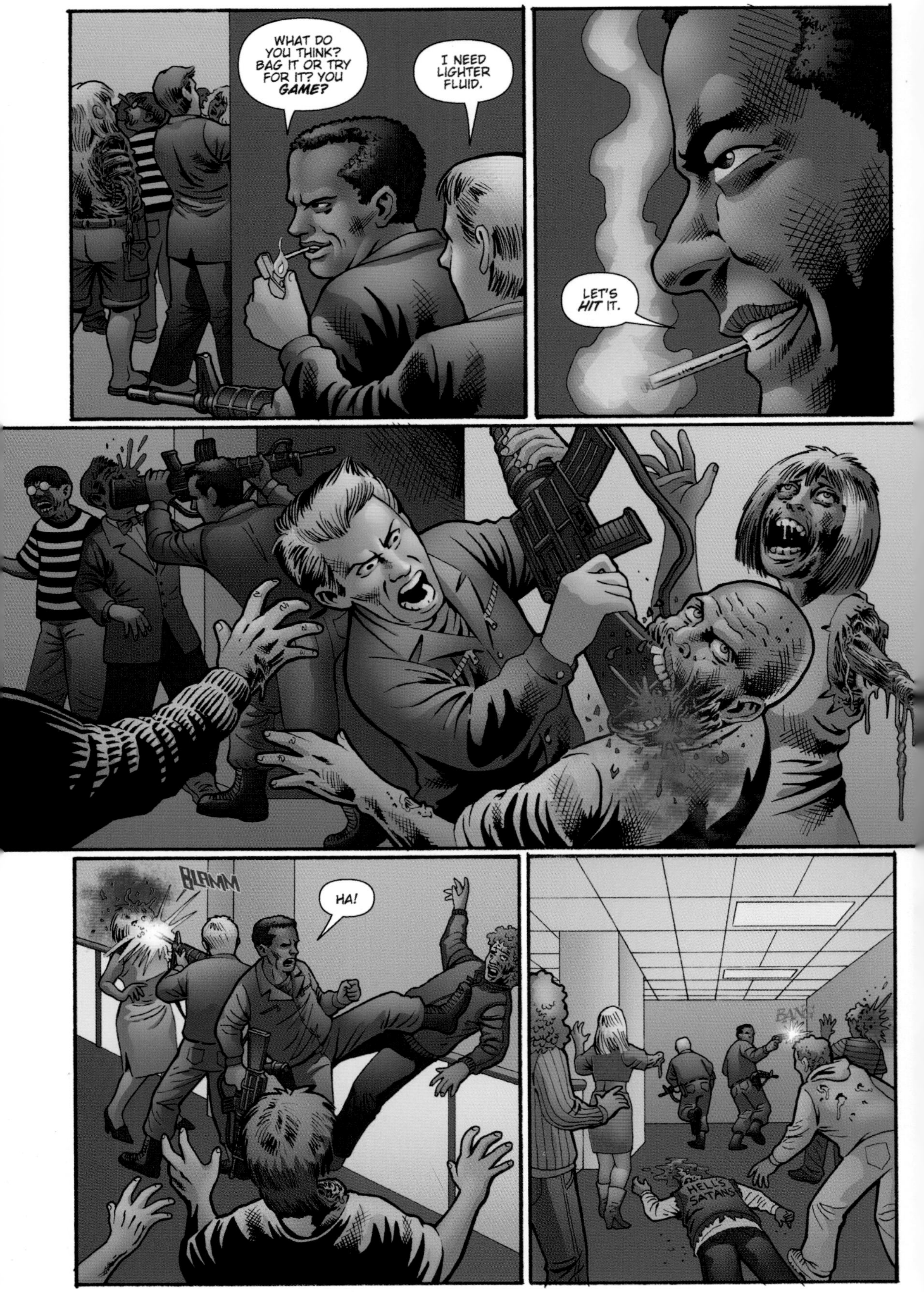

WHAT DO YOU THINK? BAG IT OR TRY FOR IT? YOU *GAME?*
I NEED LIGHTER FLUID.
LET'S *HIT* IT.
BLAMM
HA!
BANG
HELL'S SATANS

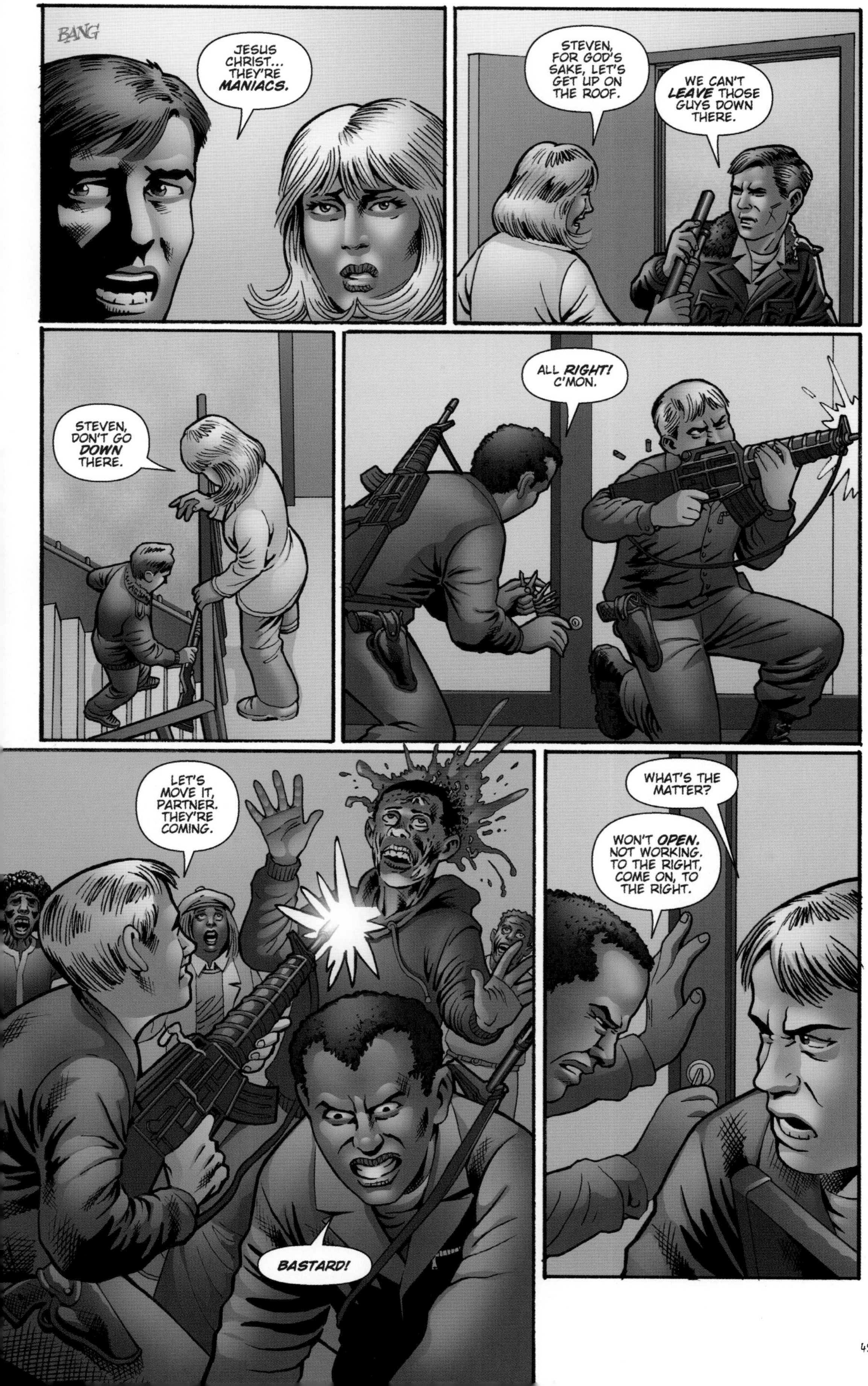
BANG
JESUS CHRIST... THEY'RE MANIACS.
STEVEN, FOR GOD'S SAKE, LET'S GET UP ON THE ROOF.
WE CAN'T LEAVE THOSE GUYS DOWN THERE.
STEVEN, DON'T GO DOWN THERE.
ALL RIGHT! C'MON.
LET'S MOVE IT, PARTNER. THEY'RE COMING.
BASTARD!
WHAT'S THE MATTER?
WON'T OPEN. NOT WORKING. TO THE RIGHT, COME ON, TO THE RIGHT.

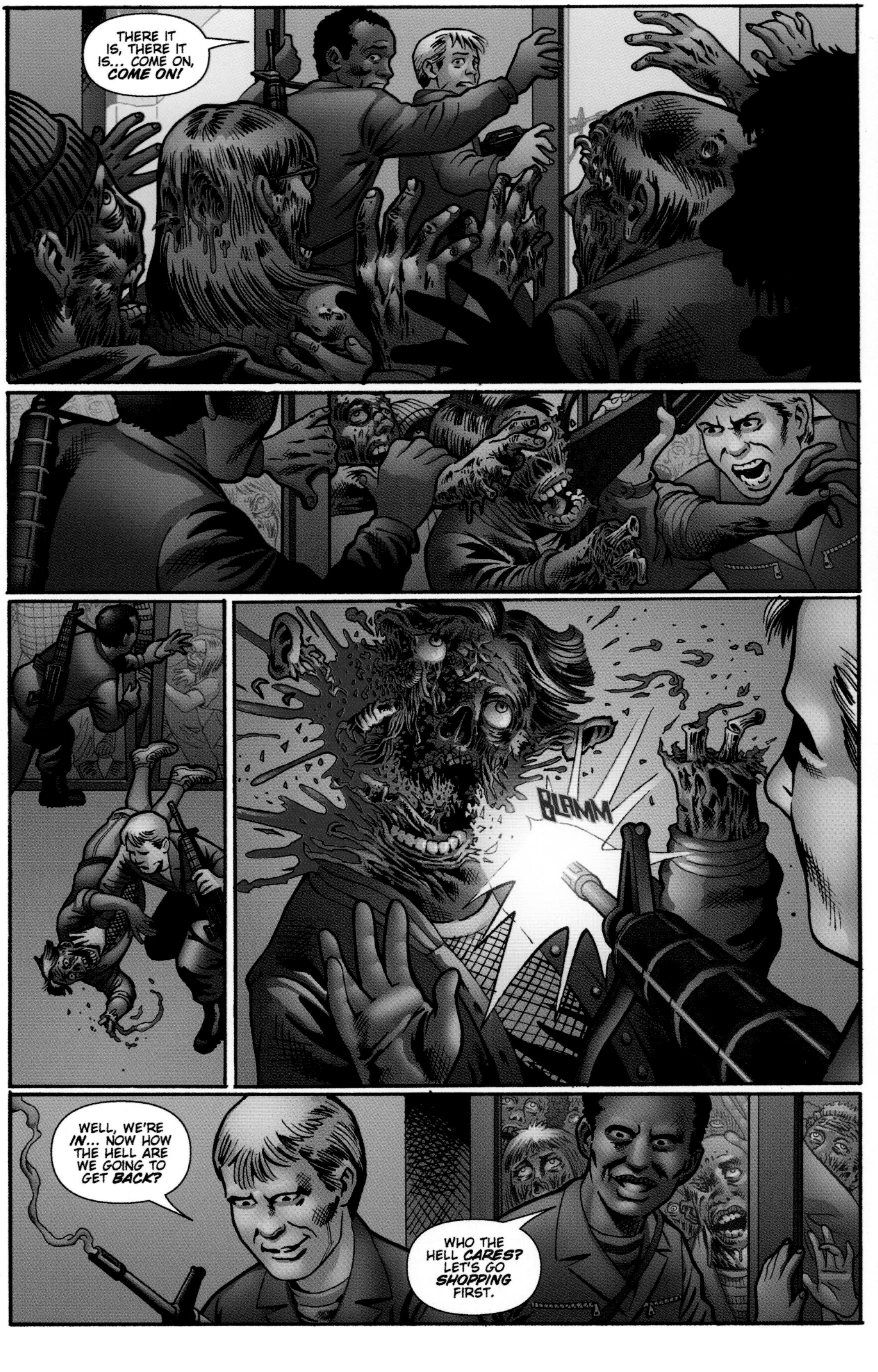
THERE IT IS, THERE IT IS... COME ON, COME ON!
BLAMM
WELL, WE'RE IN... NOW HOW THE HELL ARE WE GOING TO GET BACK?
WHO THE HELL CARES? LET'S GO SHOPPING FIRST.

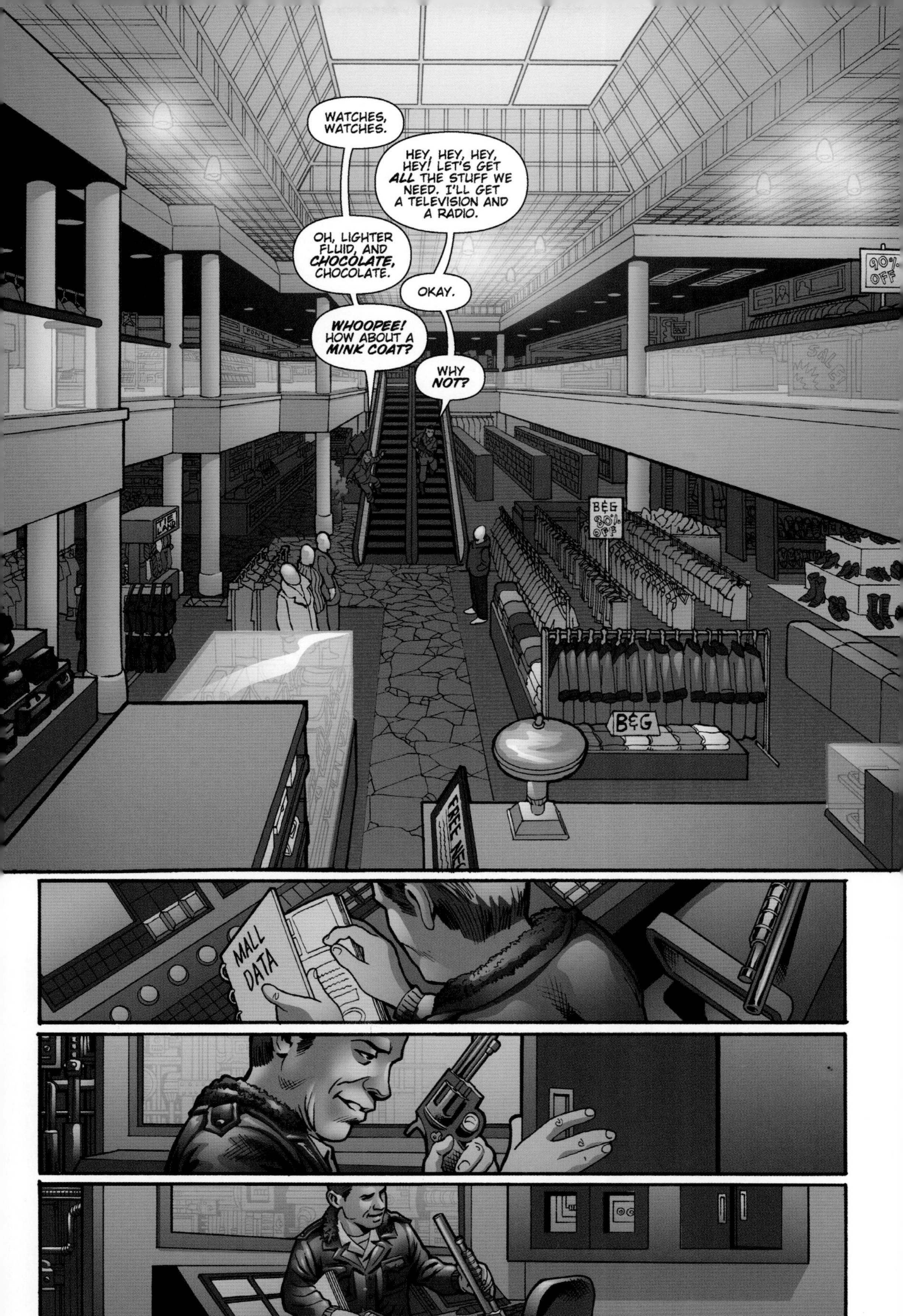
WATCHES, WATCHES.
HEY, HEY, HEY, HEY! LET'S GET ALL THE STUFF WE NEED. I'LL GET A TELEVISION AND A RADIO.
OH, LIGHTER FLUID, AND CHOCOLATE, CHOCOLATE.
OKAY.
WHOOPEE! HOW ABOUT A MINK COAT?
WHY NOT?
90% OFF
B&G 30% OFF
B&G
MALL DATA

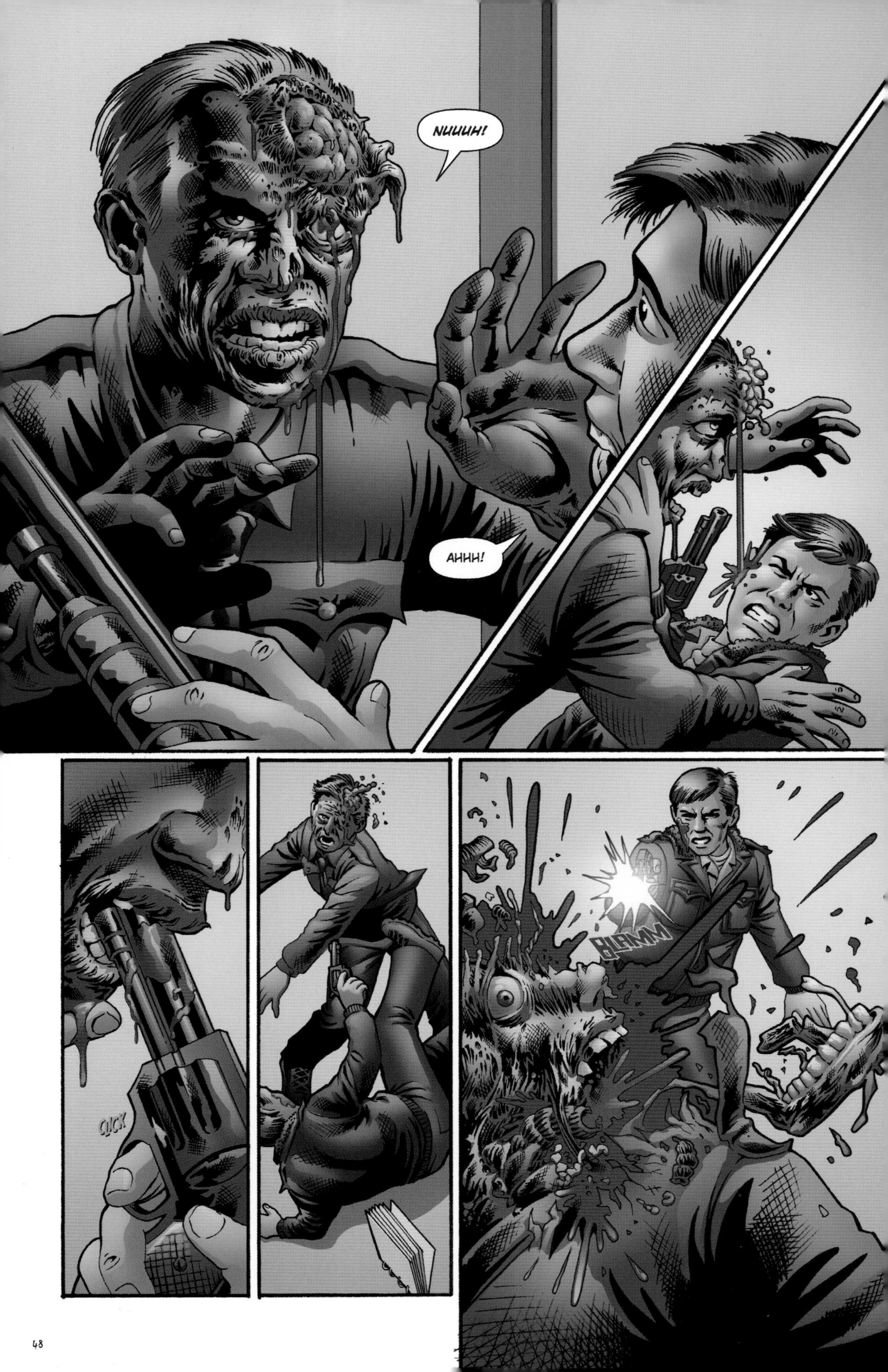

NUUUH!
AHHH!
CLICK
BLAMM

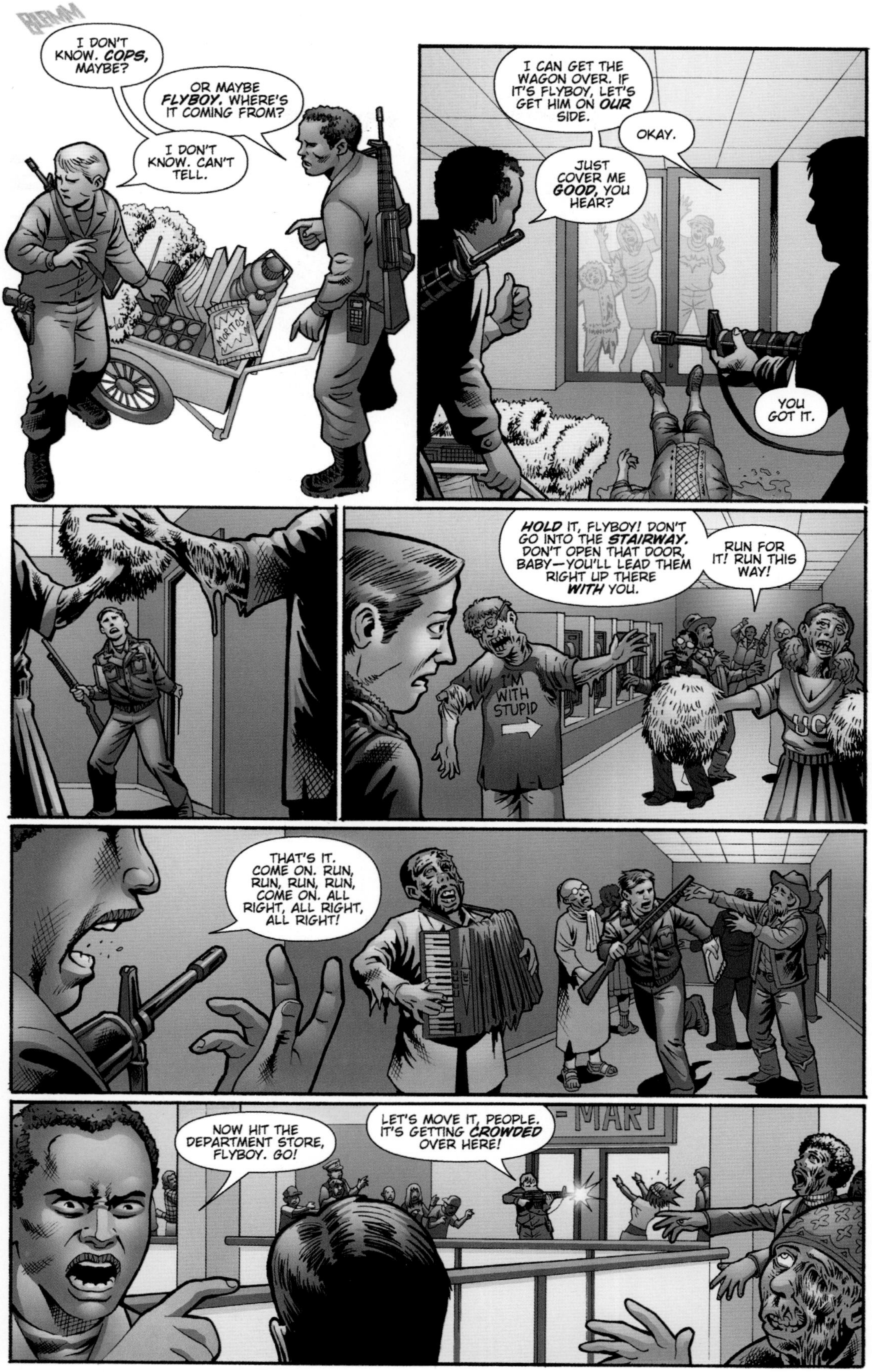
I DON'T KNOW. COPS, MAYBE?
OR MAYBE FLYBOY. WHERE'S IT COMING FROM?
I DON'T KNOW. CAN'T TELL.
MORITOS
I CAN GET THE WAGON OVER. IF IT'S FLYBOY, LET'S GET HIM ON OUR SIDE.
OKAY.
JUST COVER ME GOOD, YOU HEAR?
YOU GOT IT.
HOLD IT, FLYBOY! DON'T GO INTO THE STAIRWAY. DON'T OPEN THAT DOOR, BABY—YOU'LL LEAD THEM RIGHT UP THERE WITH YOU.
RUN FOR IT! RUN THIS WAY!
I'M WITH STUPID
THAT'S IT. COME ON. RUN, RUN, RUN, RUN, COME ON. ALL RIGHT, ALL RIGHT, ALL RIGHT!
NOW HIT THE DEPARTMENT STORE, FLYBOY. GO!
LET'S MOVE IT, PEOPLE. IT'S GETTING CROWDED OVER HERE!

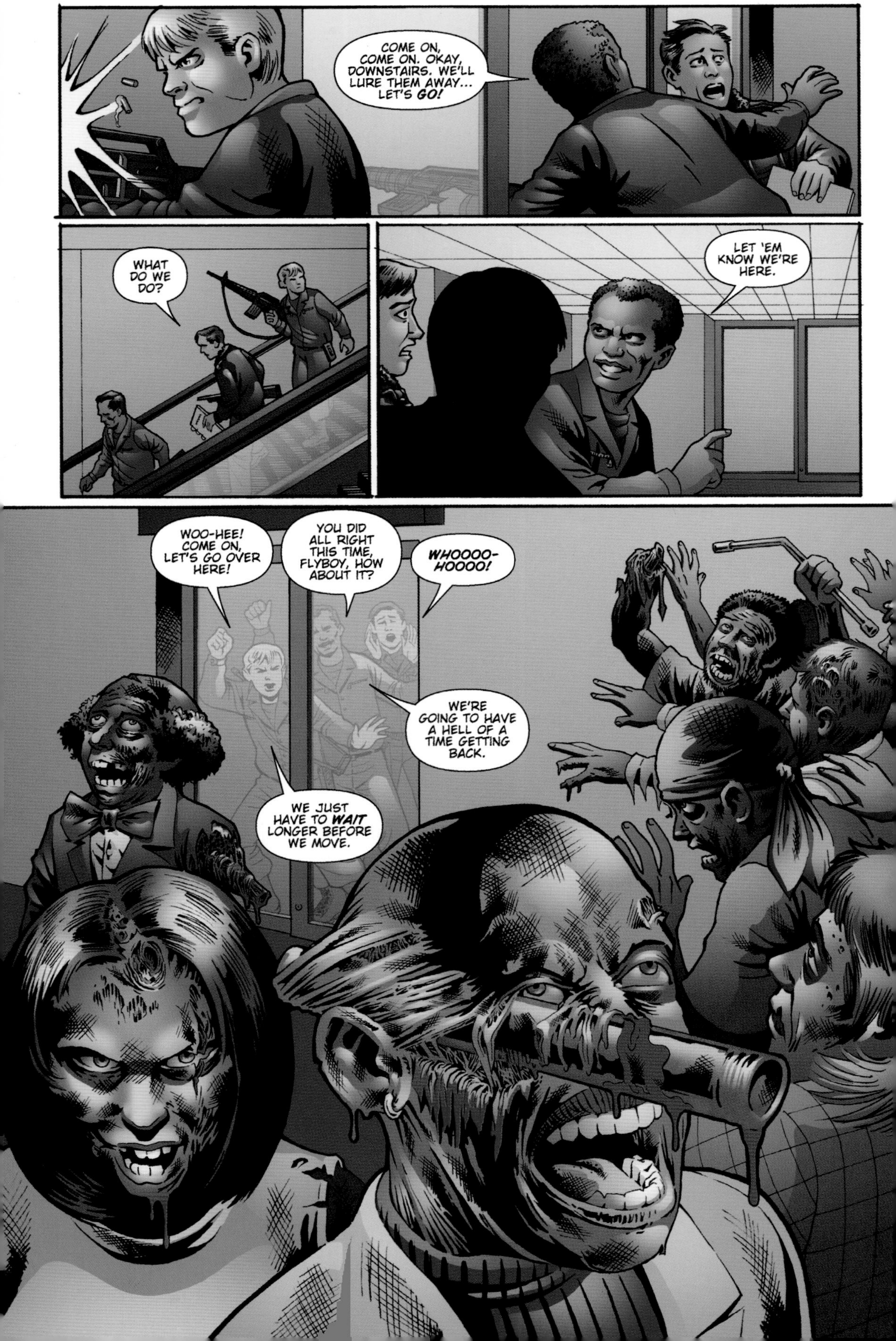
COME ON, COME ON. OKAY, DOWNSTAIRS. WE'LL LURE THEM AWAY... LET'S GO!
WHAT DO WE DO?
LET 'EM KNOW WE'RE HERE.
WOO-HEE! COME ON, LET'S GO OVER HERE!
YOU DID ALL RIGHT THIS TIME, FLYBOY, HOW ABOUT IT?
WHOOOO-HOOOO!
WE'RE GOING TO HAVE A HELL OF A TIME GETTING BACK.
WE JUST HAVE TO WAIT LONGER BEFORE WE MOVE.

NO, THERE'S ALWAYS A CHANCE OF SOME OF THEM STAYING UP ON THE BALCONY.

WE CAN HANDLE THAT. WE CAN BREAK *THROUGH* THEM.

IF ANY OF THEM SEE US, OR HEAR US, THEY'LL JUST FOLLOW US ON UP. IT'S *NO GOOD.*

I'VE BEEN THINKING. MAYBE WE GOT A *GOOD THING* GOING HERE. MAYBE WE SHOULDN'T BE IN SUCH A HURRY TO *LEAVE.*

WHAT ARE YOU SAYING?

IF WE CAN GET BACK UP THERE WITHOUT THEM CATCHING ON, WE CAN HOLE UP FOR A WHILE. AT LEAST LONG ENOUGH TO CATCH A BREATH... CHECK OUT THE RADIO, SEE WHAT'S HAPPENING.

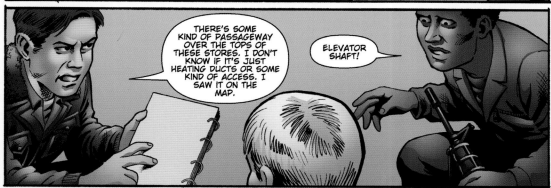

THERE'S SOME KIND OF PASSAGEWAY OVER THE TOPS OF THESE STORES. I DON'T KNOW IF IT'S JUST HEATING DUCTS OR SOME KIND OF ACCESS. I SAW IT ON THE MAP.

ELEVATOR SHAFT!

HOLD THE DOORS. IT'S HERE. YOU *FOUND* IT, FLYBOY.

A GUN SHOP!

KEEP *MOVING,* SPORT. I SAW IT.

51

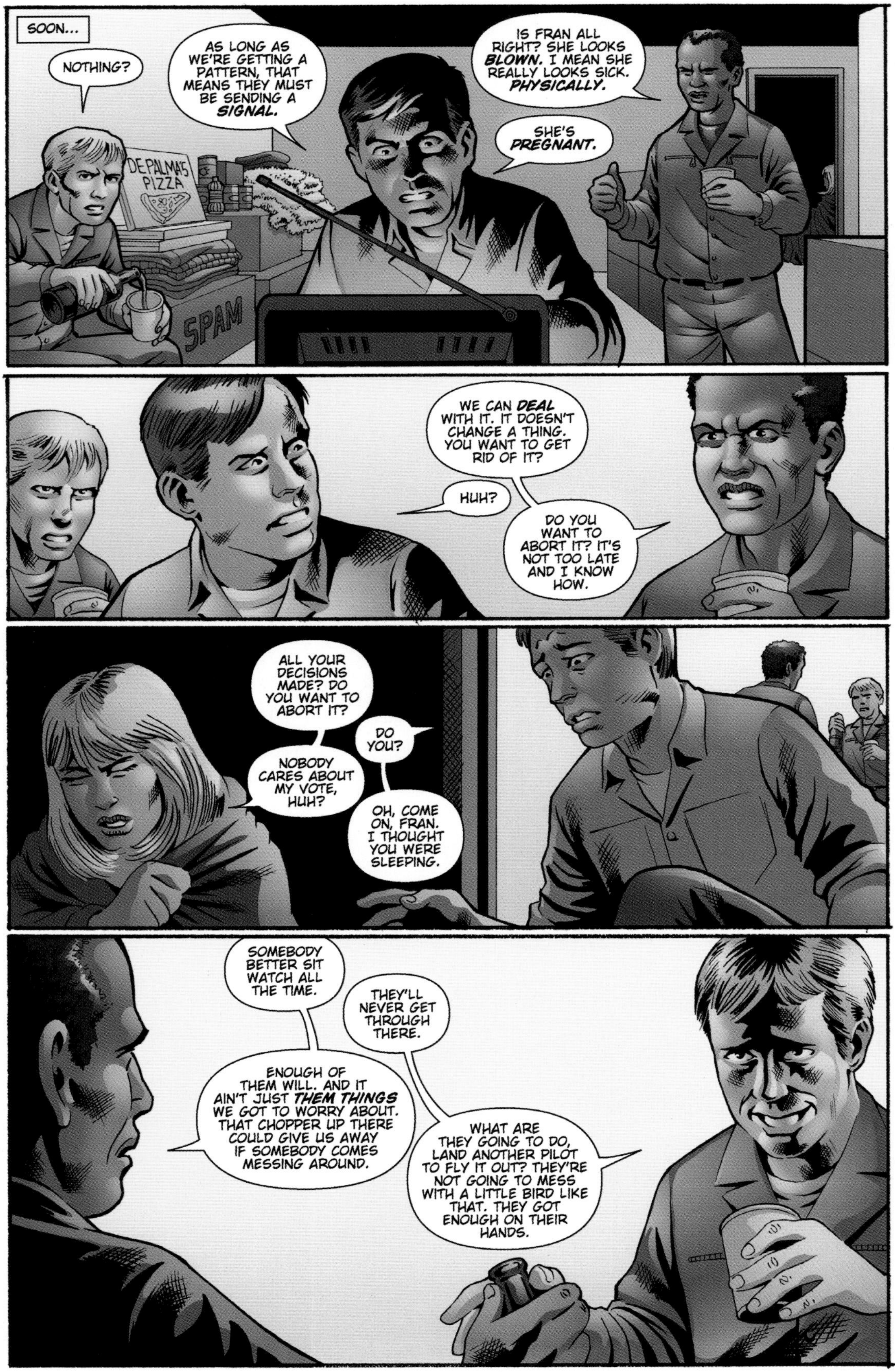
SOON...
NOTHING?
AS LONG AS WE'RE GETTING A PATTERN, THAT MEANS THEY MUST BE SENDING A SIGNAL.
IS FRAN ALL RIGHT? SHE LOOKS BLOWN. I MEAN SHE REALLY LOOKS SICK. PHYSICALLY.
SHE'S PREGNANT.
DEPALMA'S PIZZA
SPAM
WE CAN DEAL WITH IT. IT DOESN'T CHANGE A THING. YOU WANT TO GET RID OF IT?
HUH?
DO YOU WANT TO ABORT IT? IT'S NOT TOO LATE AND I KNOW HOW.
ALL YOUR DECISIONS MADE? DO YOU WANT TO ABORT IT?
NOBODY CARES ABOUT MY VOTE, HUH?
DO YOU?
OH, COME ON, FRAN. I THOUGHT YOU WERE SLEEPING.
SOMEBODY BETTER SIT WATCH ALL THE TIME.
THEY'LL NEVER GET THROUGH THERE.
ENOUGH OF THEM WILL. AND IT AIN'T JUST THEM THINGS WE GOT TO WORRY ABOUT. THAT CHOPPER UP THERE COULD GIVE US AWAY IF SOMEBODY COMES MESSING AROUND.
WHAT ARE THEY GOING TO DO, LAND ANOTHER PILOT TO FLY IT OUT? THEY'RE NOT GOING TO MESS WITH A LITTLE BIRD LIKE THAT. THEY GOT ENOUGH ON THEIR HANDS.

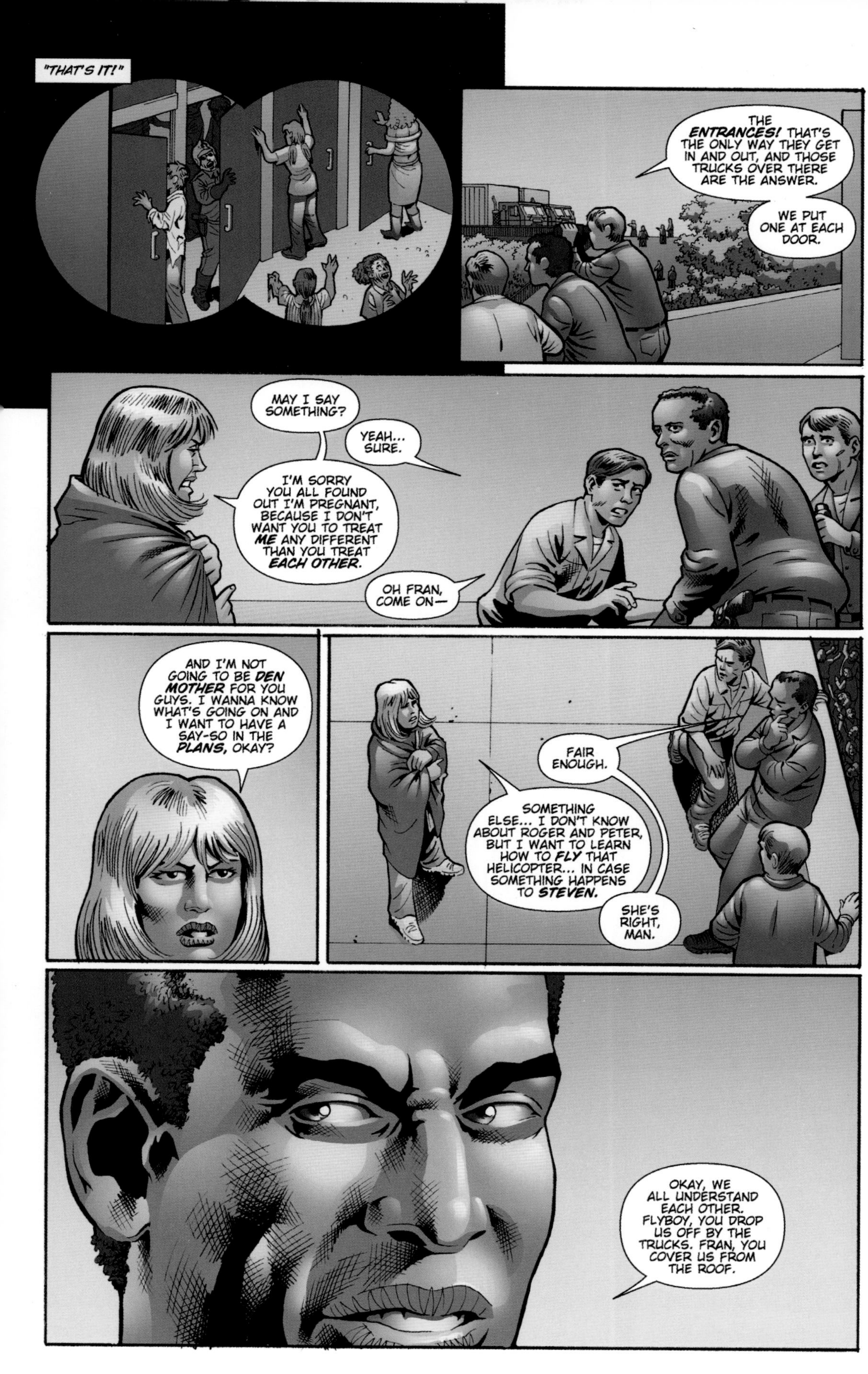
"THAT'S IT!"
THE ENTRANCES! THAT'S THE ONLY WAY THEY GET IN AND OUT, AND THOSE TRUCKS OVER THERE ARE THE ANSWER.
WE PUT ONE AT EACH DOOR.
MAY I SAY SOMETHING?
YEAH... SURE.
I'M SORRY YOU ALL FOUND OUT I'M PREGNANT, BECAUSE I DON'T WANT YOU TO TREAT ME ANY DIFFERENT THAN YOU TREAT EACH OTHER.
OH FRAN, COME ON—
AND I'M NOT GOING TO BE DEN MOTHER FOR YOU GUYS. I WANNA KNOW WHAT'S GOING ON AND I WANT TO HAVE A SAY-SO IN THE PLANS, OKAY?
FAIR ENOUGH.
SOMETHING ELSE... I DON'T KNOW ABOUT ROGER AND PETER, BUT I WANT TO LEARN HOW TO FLY THAT HELICOPTER... IN CASE SOMETHING HAPPENS TO STEVEN.
SHE'S RIGHT, MAN.
OKAY, WE ALL UNDERSTAND EACH OTHER. FLYBOY, YOU DROP US OFF BY THE TRUCKS. FRAN, YOU COVER US FROM THE ROOF.

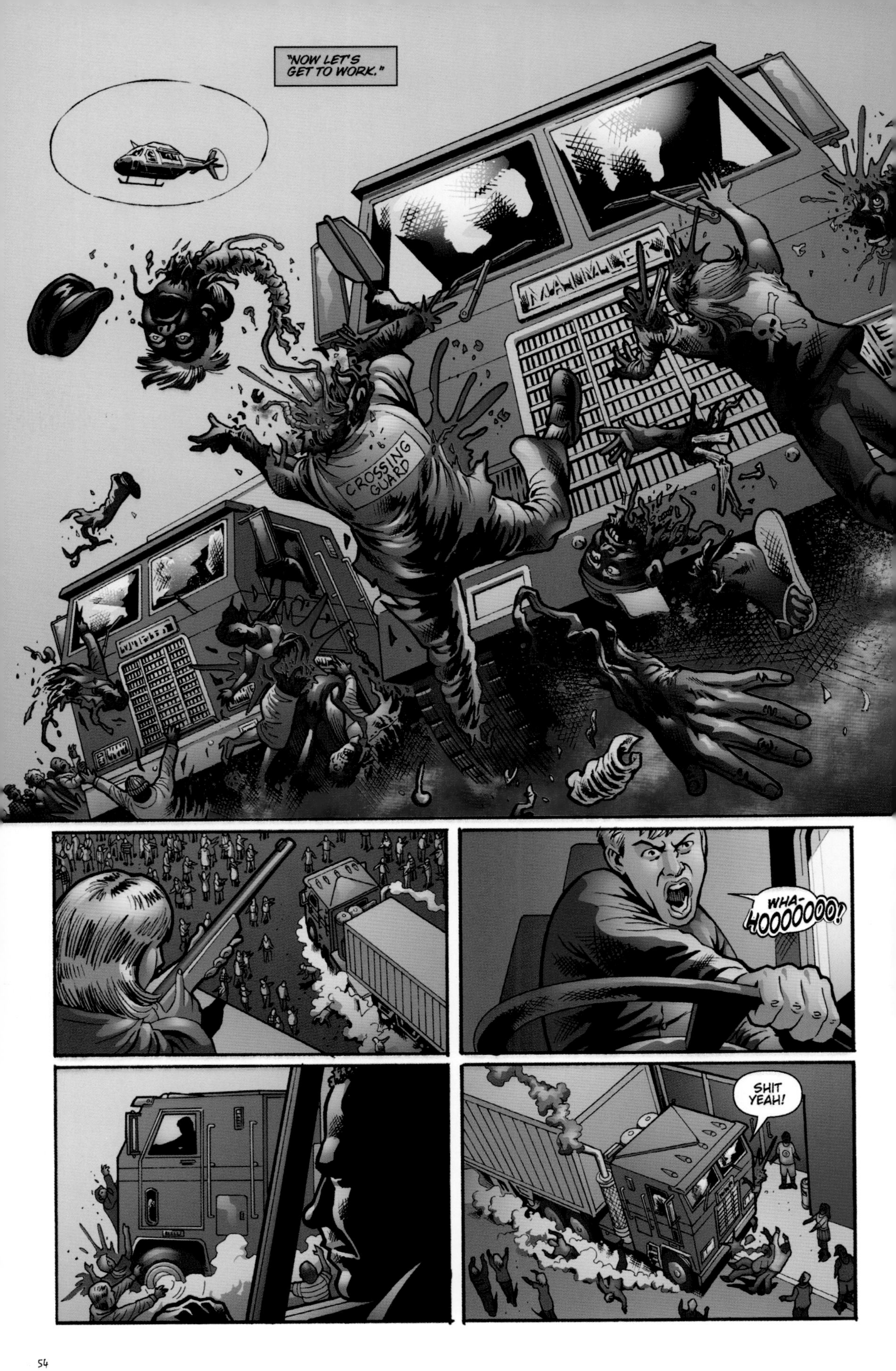
"NOW LET'S GET TO WORK."
CROSSING GUARD
WHA-HOOOOOOO!
SHIT YEAH!

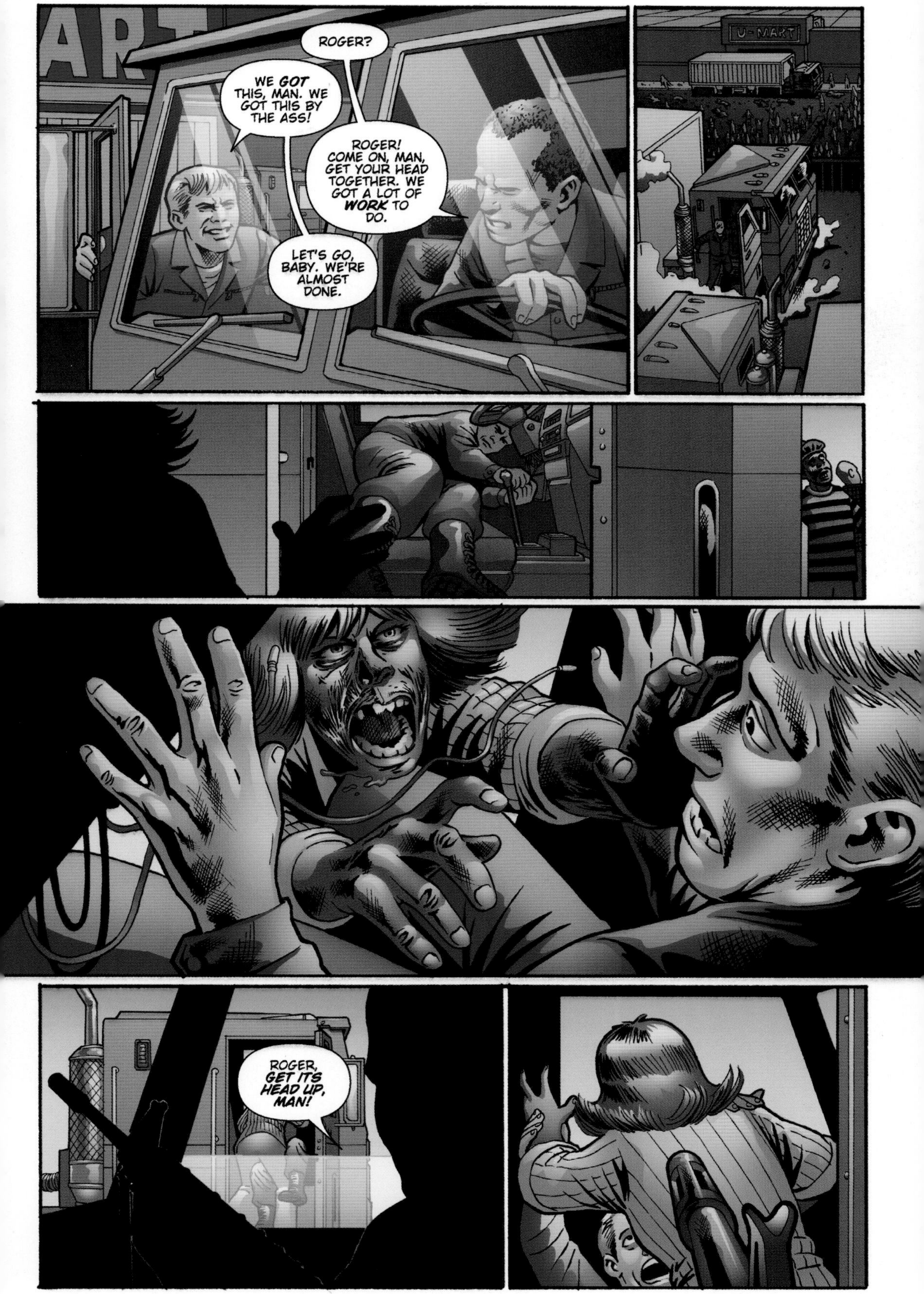
WE GOT THIS, MAN. WE GOT THIS BY THE ASS!
ROGER?
ROGER! COME ON, MAN, GET YOUR HEAD TOGETHER. WE GOT A LOT OF WORK TO DO.
LET'S GO, BABY. WE'RE ALMOST DONE.
U-MART
ROGER, GET ITS HEAD UP, MAN!

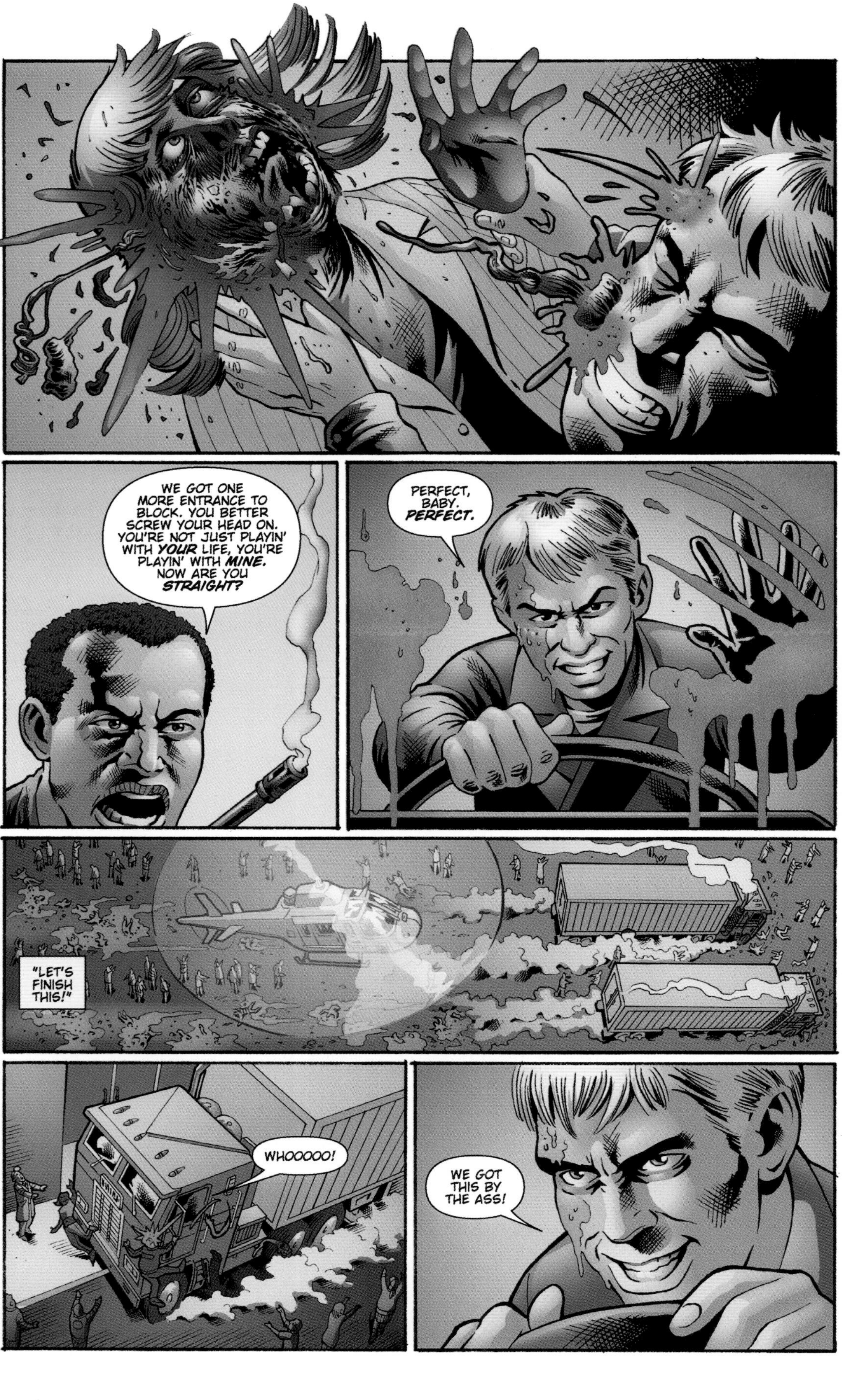
WE GOT ONE MORE ENTRANCE TO BLOCK. YOU BETTER SCREW YOUR HEAD ON. YOU'RE NOT JUST PLAYIN' WITH *YOUR* LIFE, YOU'RE PLAYIN' WITH *MINE.* NOW ARE YOU *STRAIGHT?*
PERFECT, BABY. *PERFECT.*
"LET'S FINISH THIS!"
WHOOOOO!
WE GOT THIS BY THE ASS!

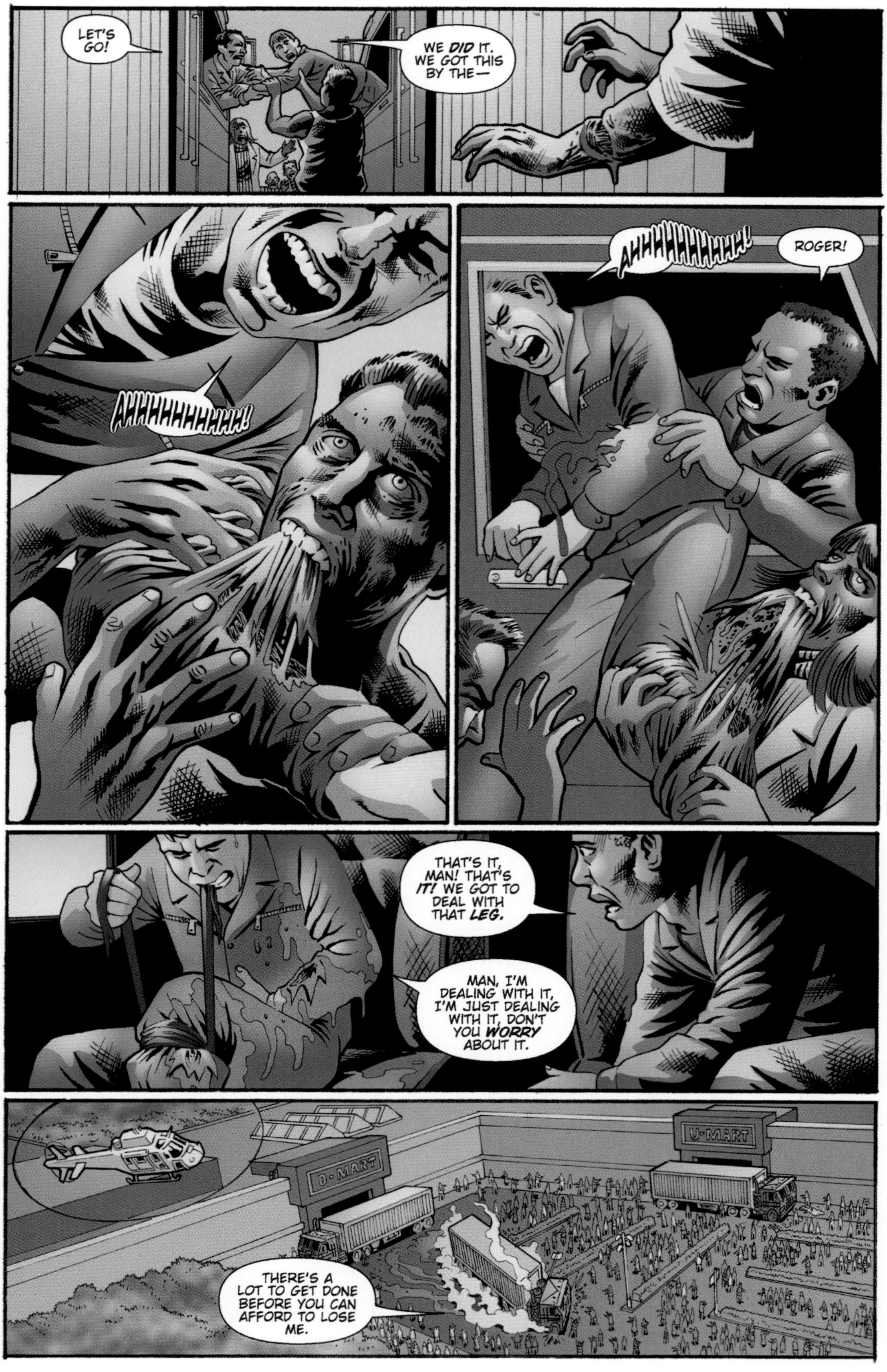
LET'S GO!
WE DID IT. WE GOT THIS BY THE—
AHHHHHHHHHH!
AHHHHHHHHHHH!
ROGER!
THAT'S IT, MAN! THAT'S IT! WE GOT TO DEAL WITH THAT LEG.
MAN, I'M DEALING WITH IT, I'M JUST DEALING WITH IT, DON'T YOU WORRY ABOUT IT.
U-MART
D-MART
THERE'S A LOT TO GET DONE BEFORE YOU CAN AFFORD TO LOSE ME.

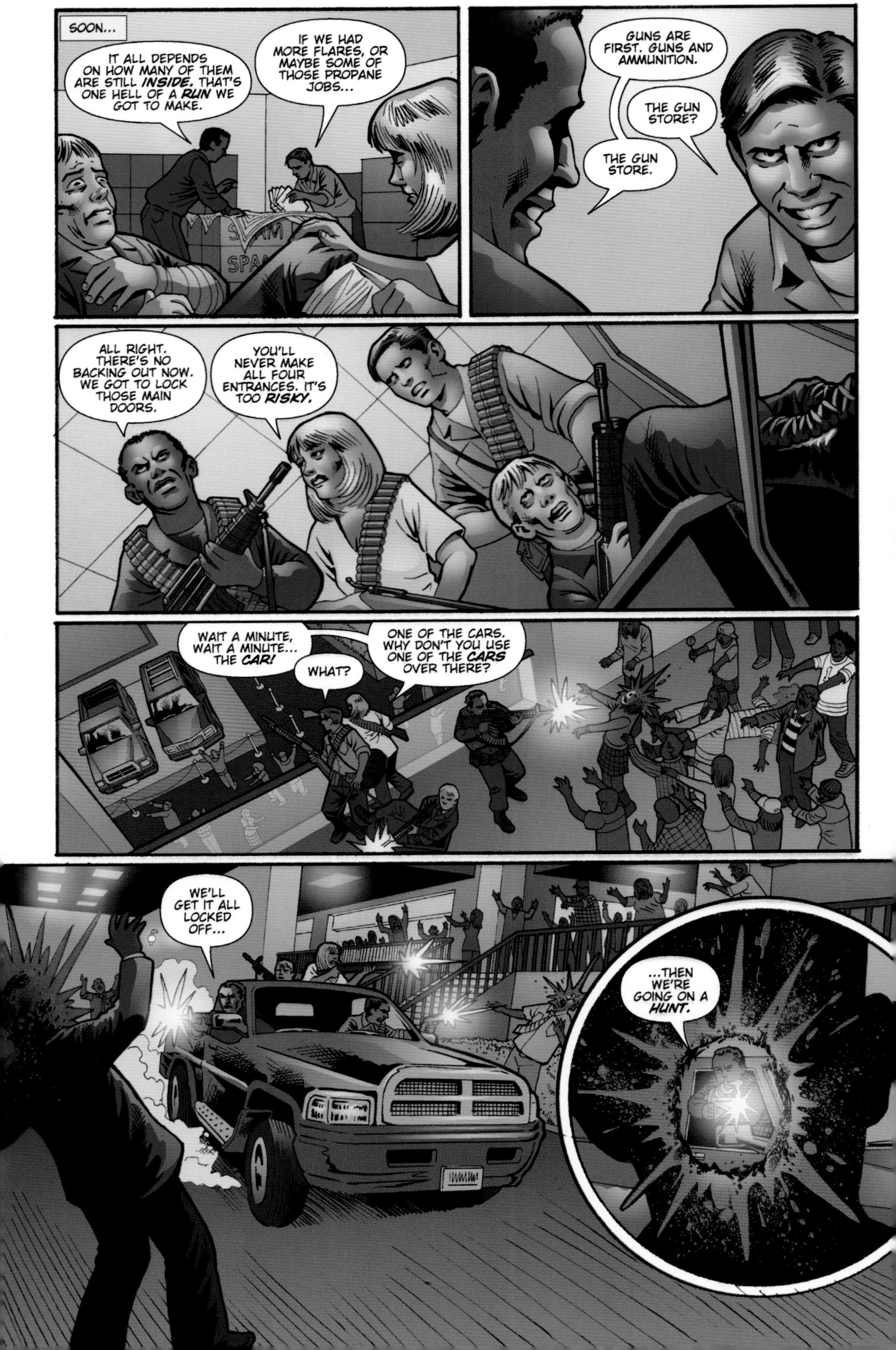
SOON...
IT ALL DEPENDS ON HOW MANY OF THEM ARE STILL INSIDE. THAT'S ONE HELL OF A RUN WE GOT TO MAKE.
IF WE HAD MORE FLARES, OR MAYBE SOME OF THOSE PROPANE JOBS...
GUNS ARE FIRST. GUNS AND AMMUNITION.
THE GUN STORE?
THE GUN STORE.
ALL RIGHT. THERE'S NO BACKING OUT NOW. WE GOT TO LOCK THOSE MAIN DOORS.
YOU'LL NEVER MAKE ALL FOUR ENTRANCES. IT'S TOO RISKY.
WAIT A MINUTE, WAIT A MINUTE... THE CAR!
WHAT?
ONE OF THE CARS. WHY DON'T YOU USE ONE OF THE CARS OVER THERE?
WE'LL GET IT ALL LOCKED OFF...
...THEN WE'RE GOING ON A HUNT.

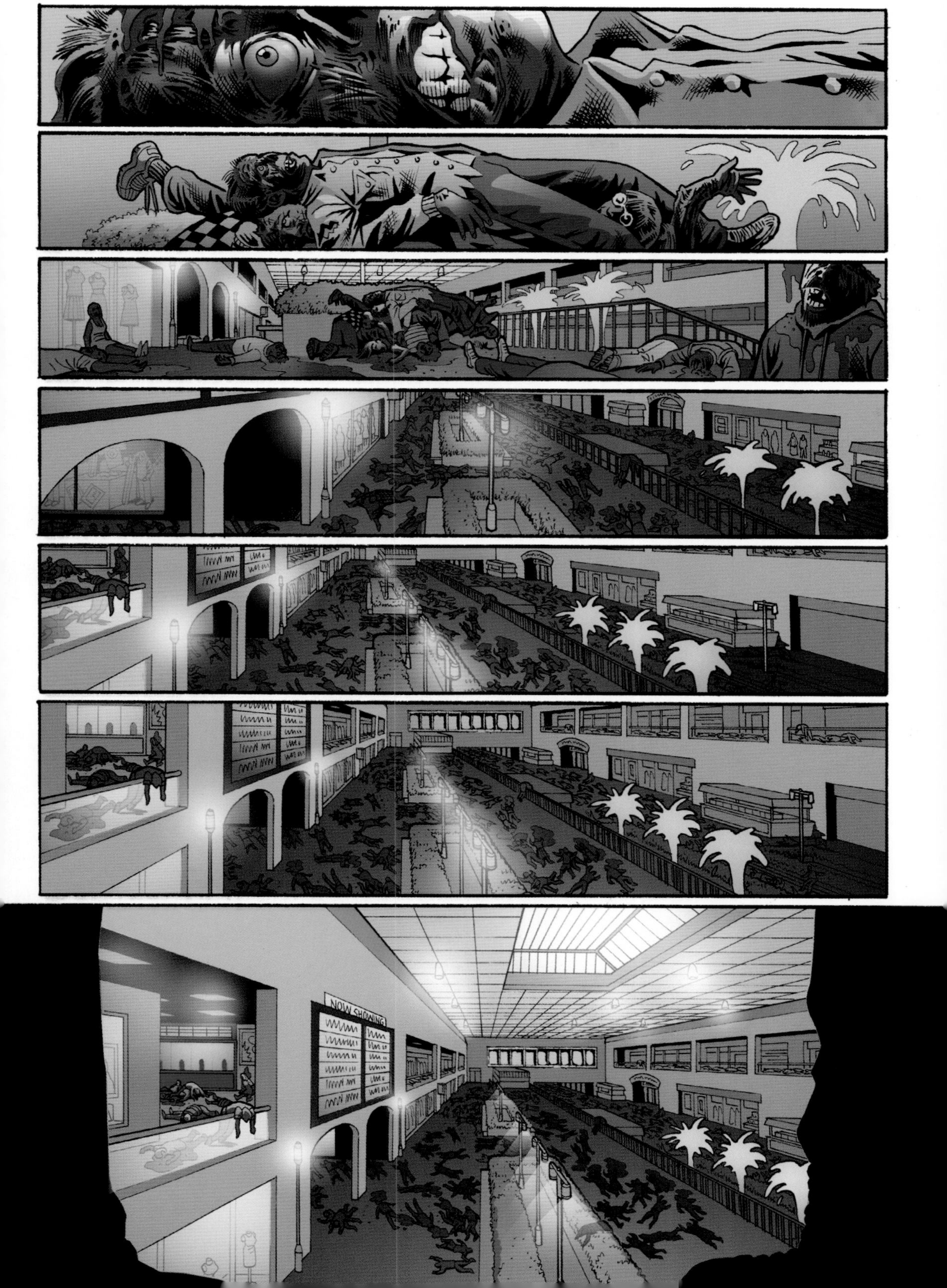
NOW SHOWING

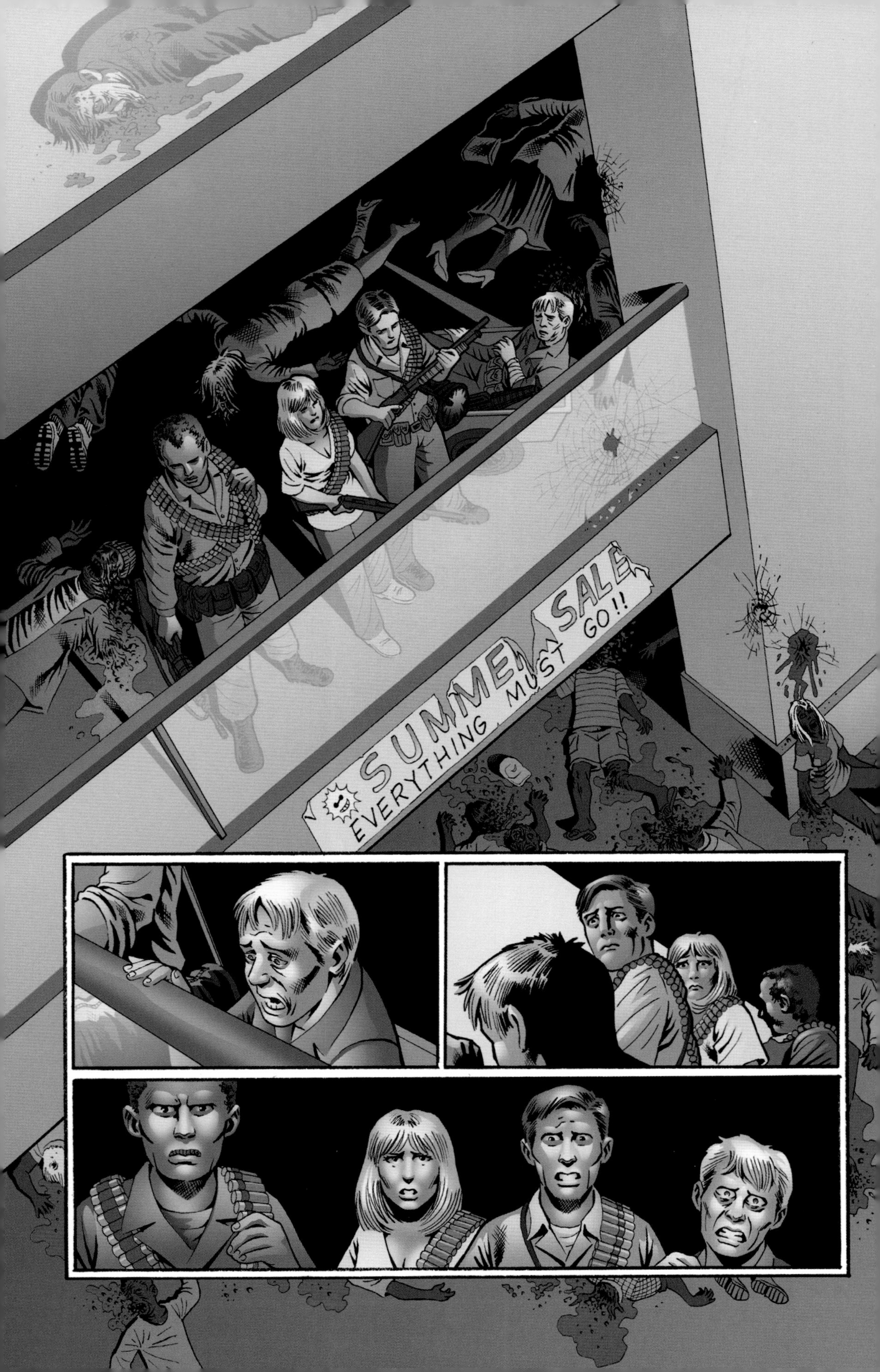
SUMME SALE
EVERYTHING MUST GO!!

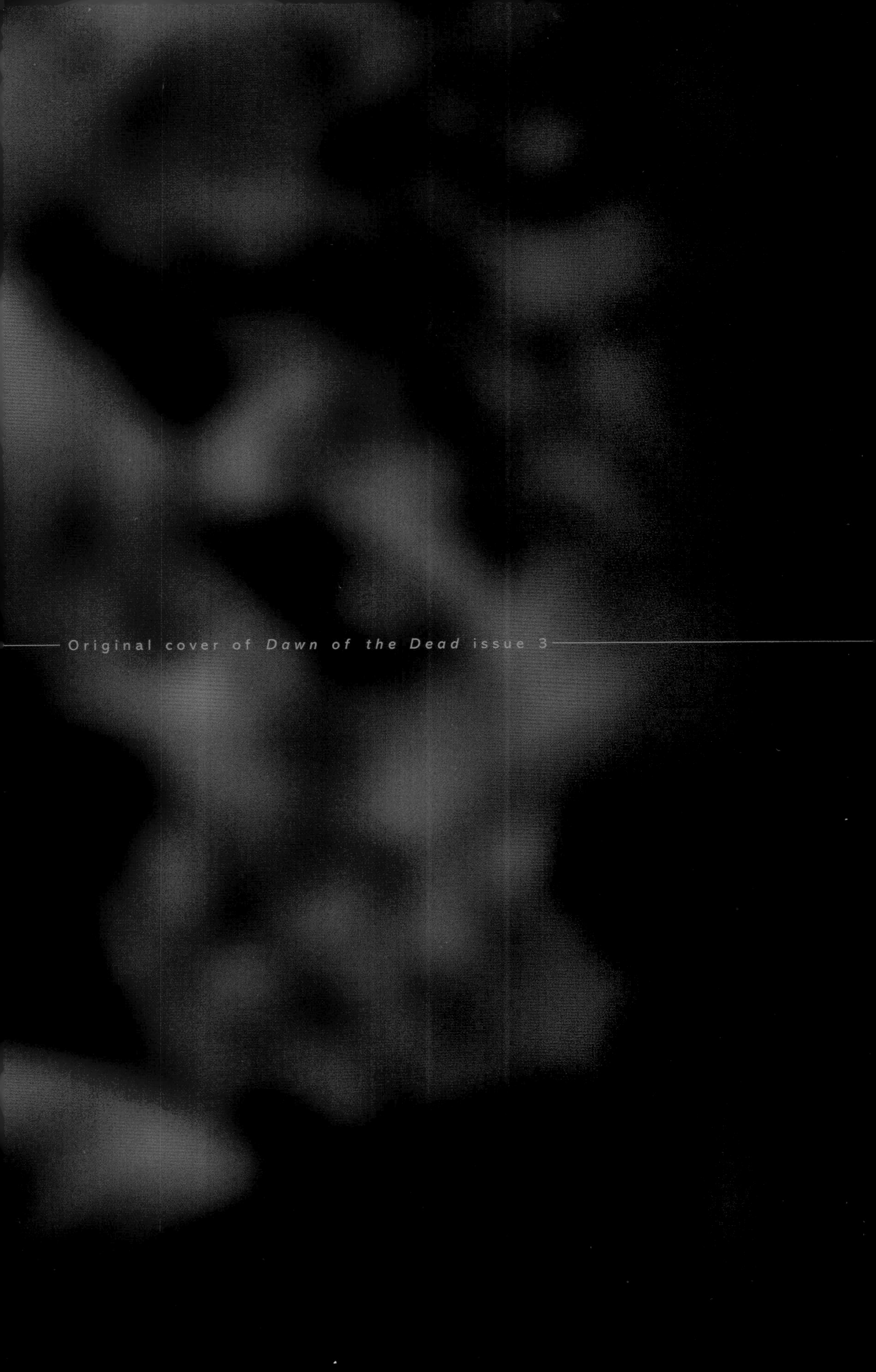

Original cover of *Dawn of the Dead* issue 3

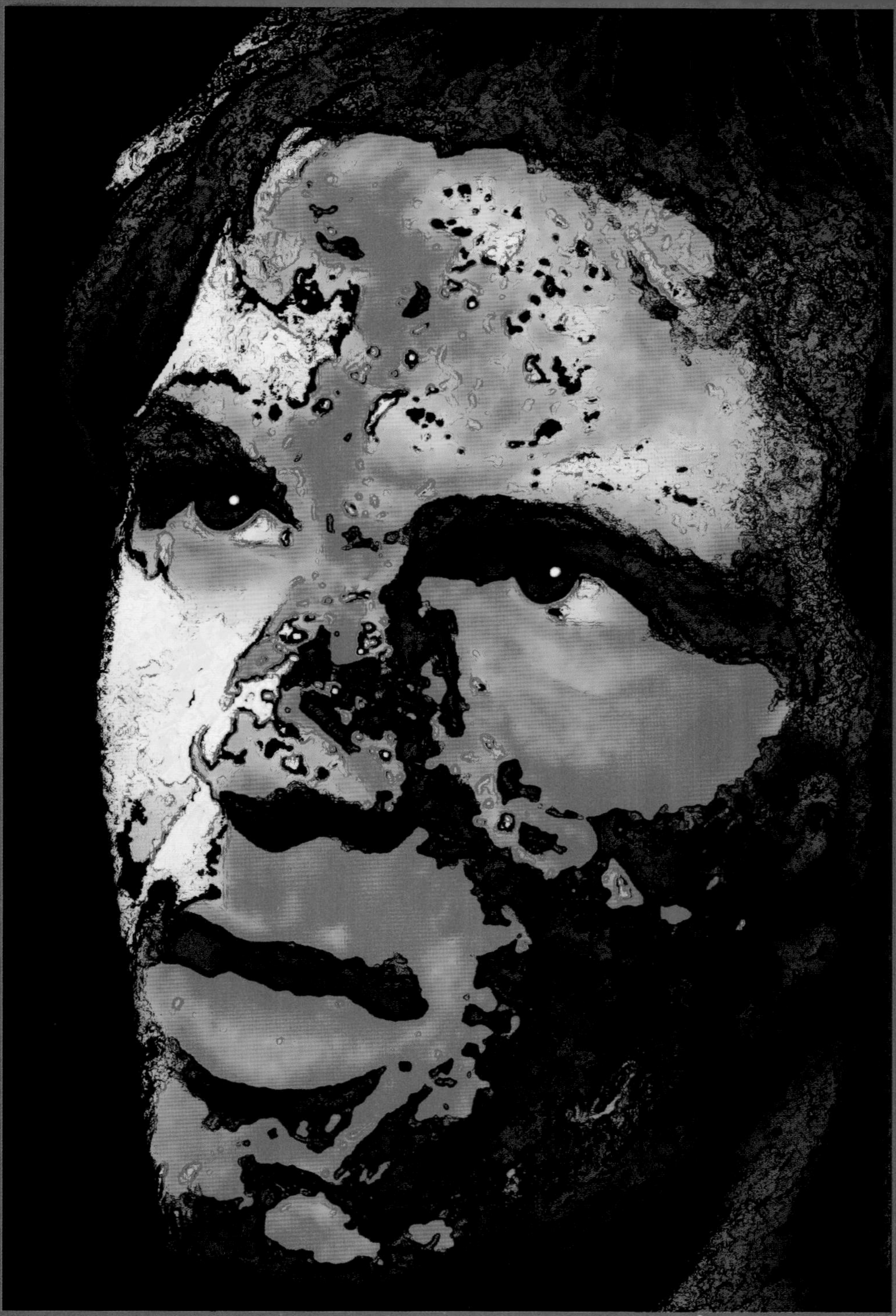

Dawn of the Dead

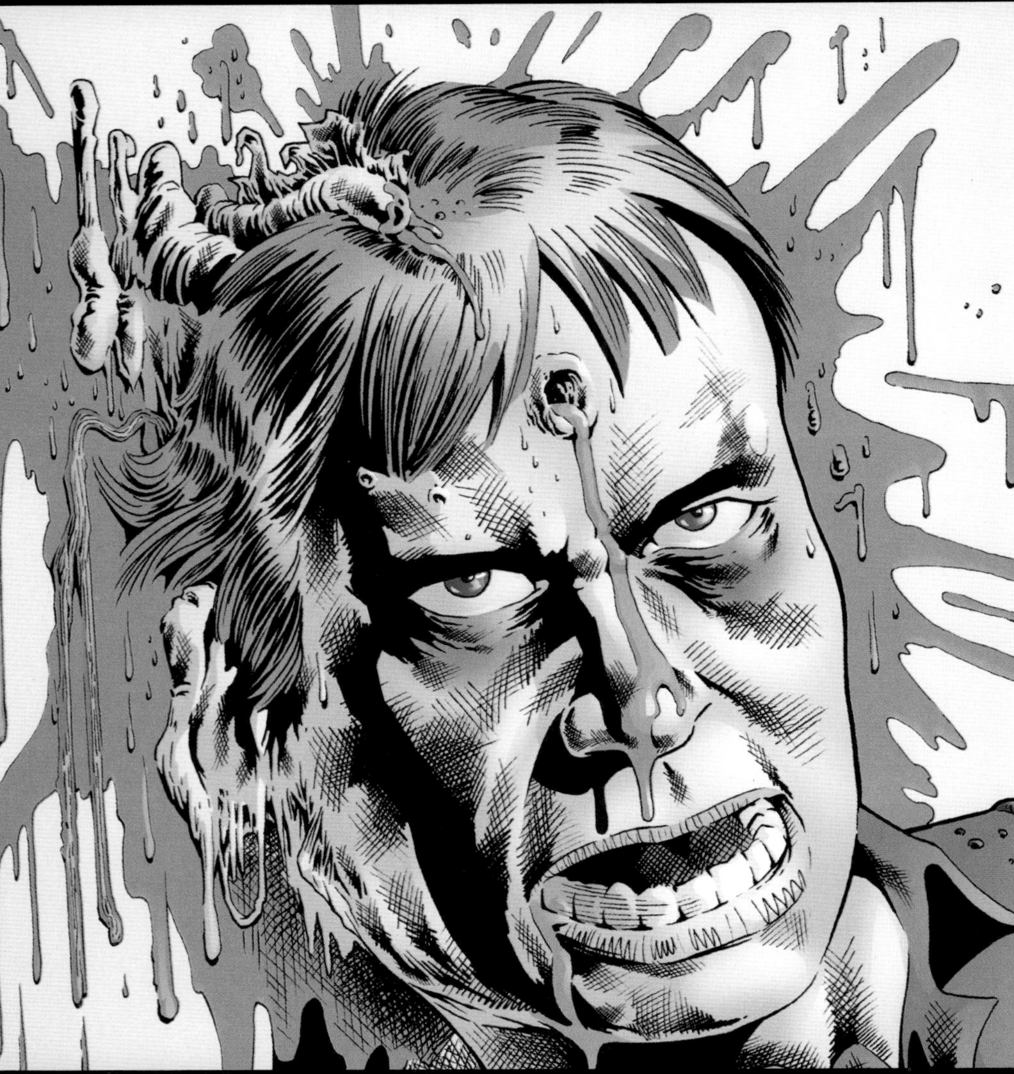

Chapter
-3-

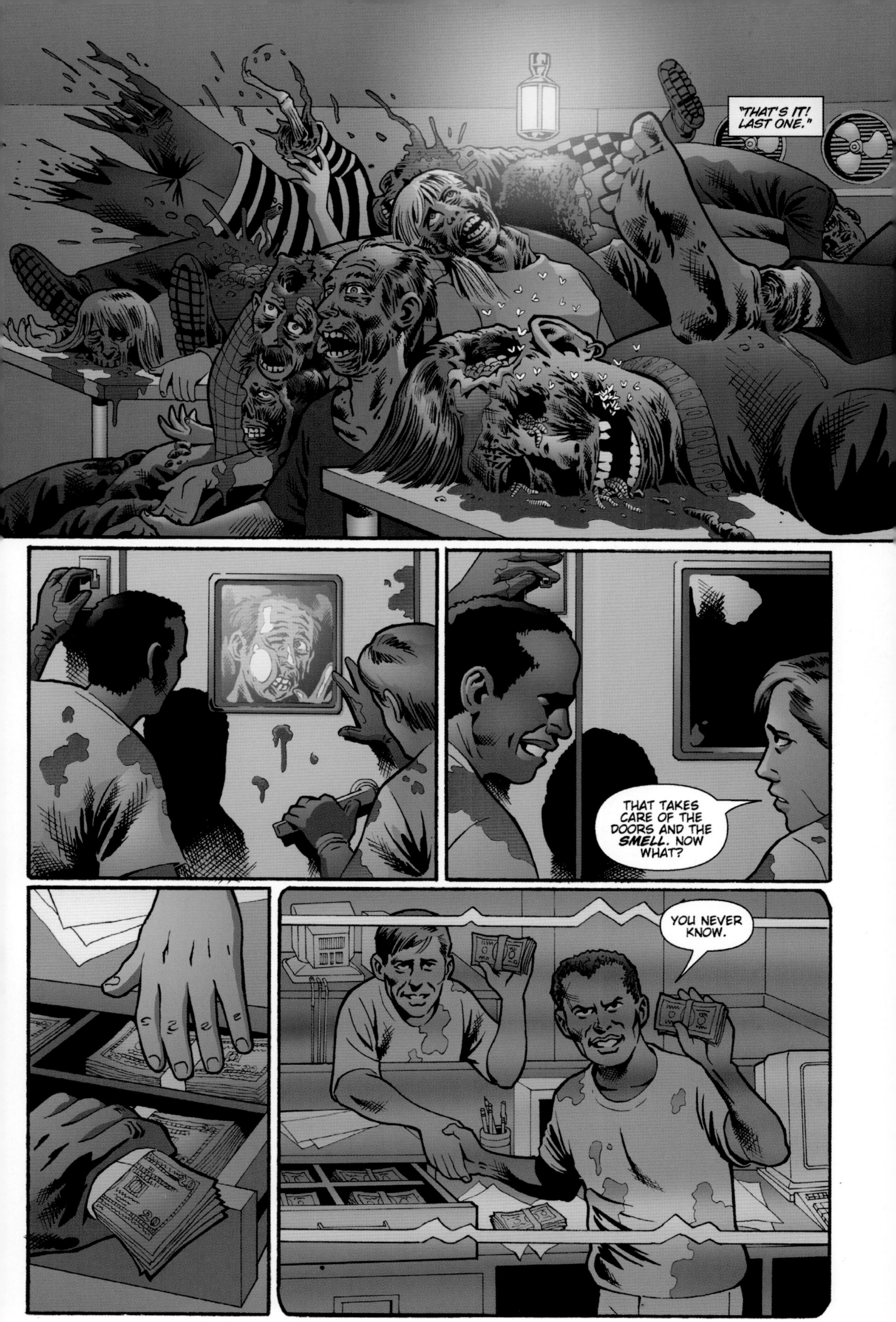
"THAT'S IT! LAST ONE."
THAT TAKES CARE OF THE DOORS AND THE SMELL. NOW WHAT?
YOU NEVER KNOW.

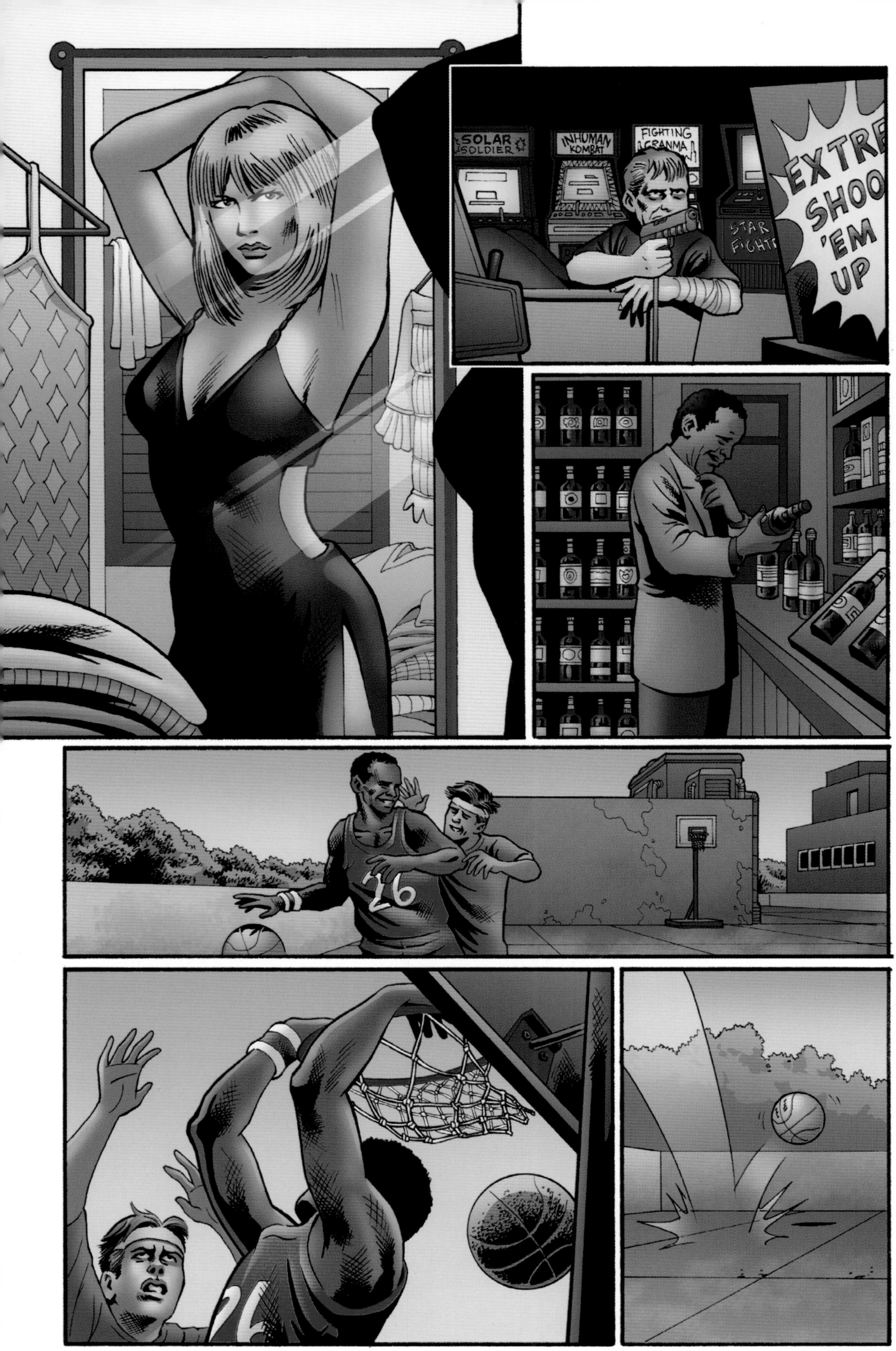
SOLAR SOLDIER
INHUMAN KOMBAT
FIGHTING GRANMA
STAR
'EM UP
26

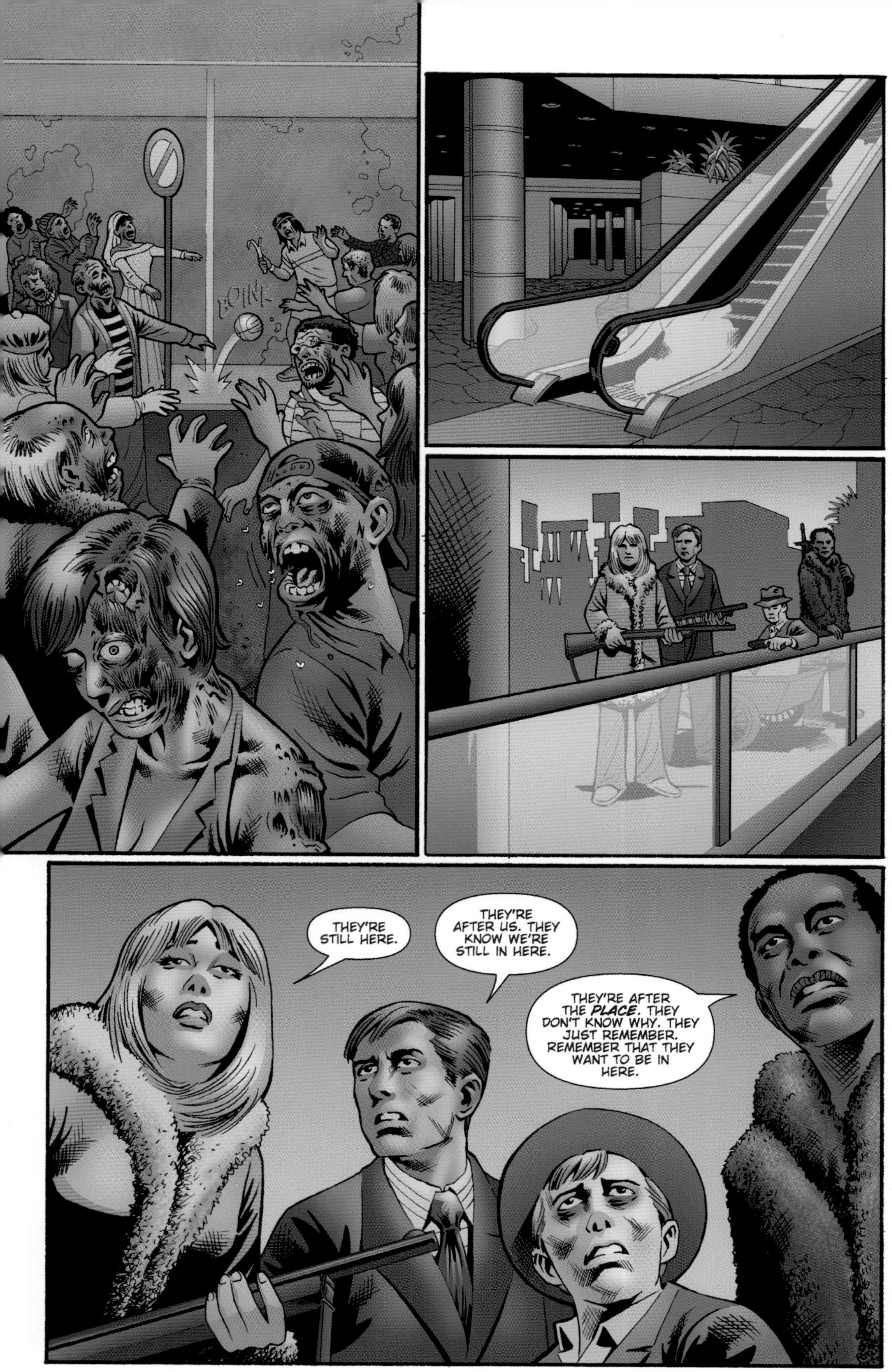
BOINK
THEY'RE STILL HERE.
THEY'RE AFTER US. THEY KNOW WE'RE STILL IN HERE.
THEY'RE AFTER THE *PLACE*. THEY DON'T KNOW WHY. THEY JUST REMEMBER. REMEMBER THAT THEY WANT TO BE IN HERE.

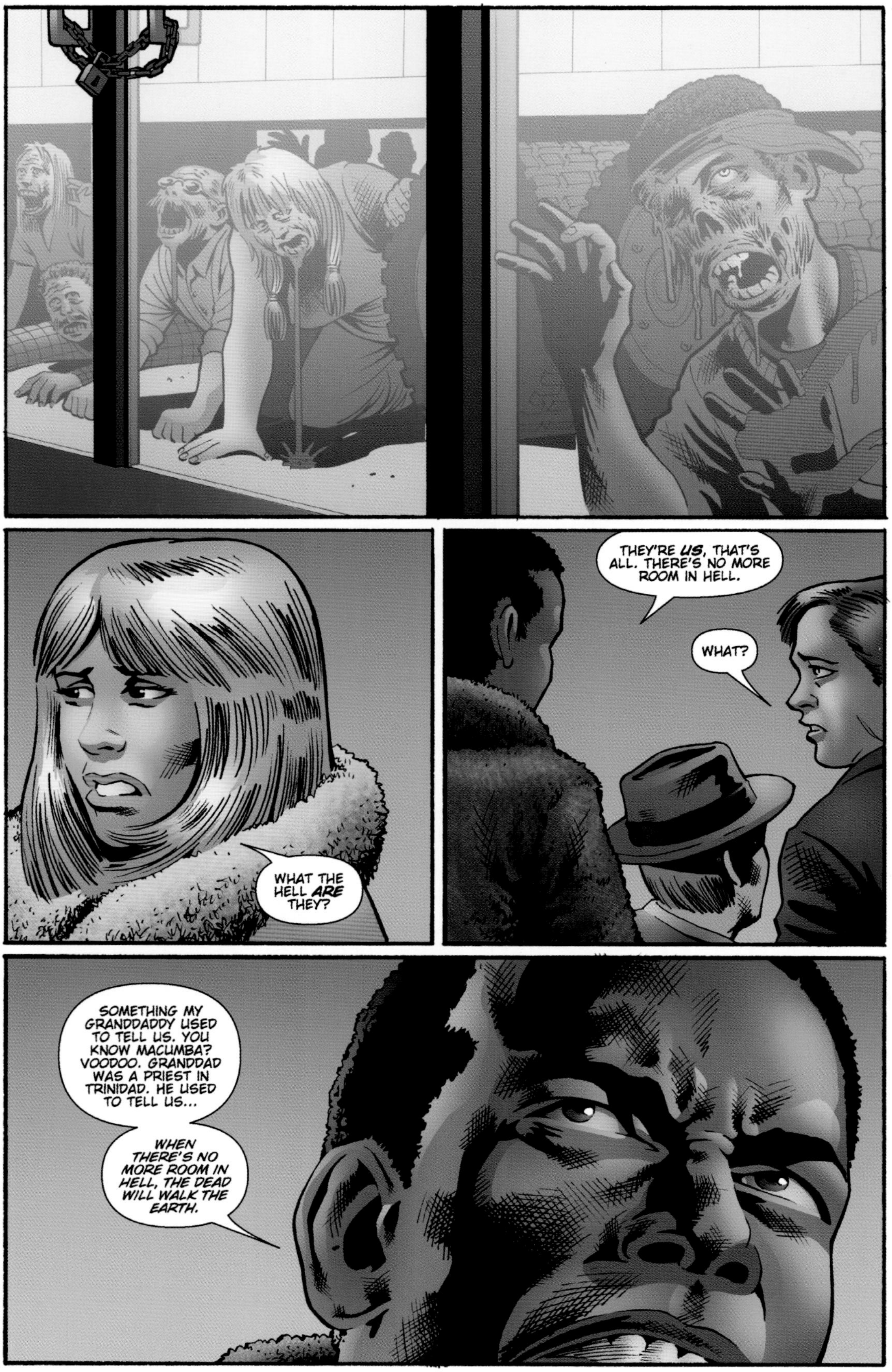
WHAT THE HELL ARE THEY?
THEY'RE US, THAT'S ALL. THERE'S NO MORE ROOM IN HELL.
WHAT?
SOMETHING MY GRANDDADDY USED TO TELL US. YOU KNOW MACUMBA? VOODOO. GRANDDAD WAS A PRIEST IN TRINIDAD. HE USED TO TELL US...
WHEN THERE'S NO MORE ROOM IN HELL, THE DEAD WILL WALK THE EARTH.

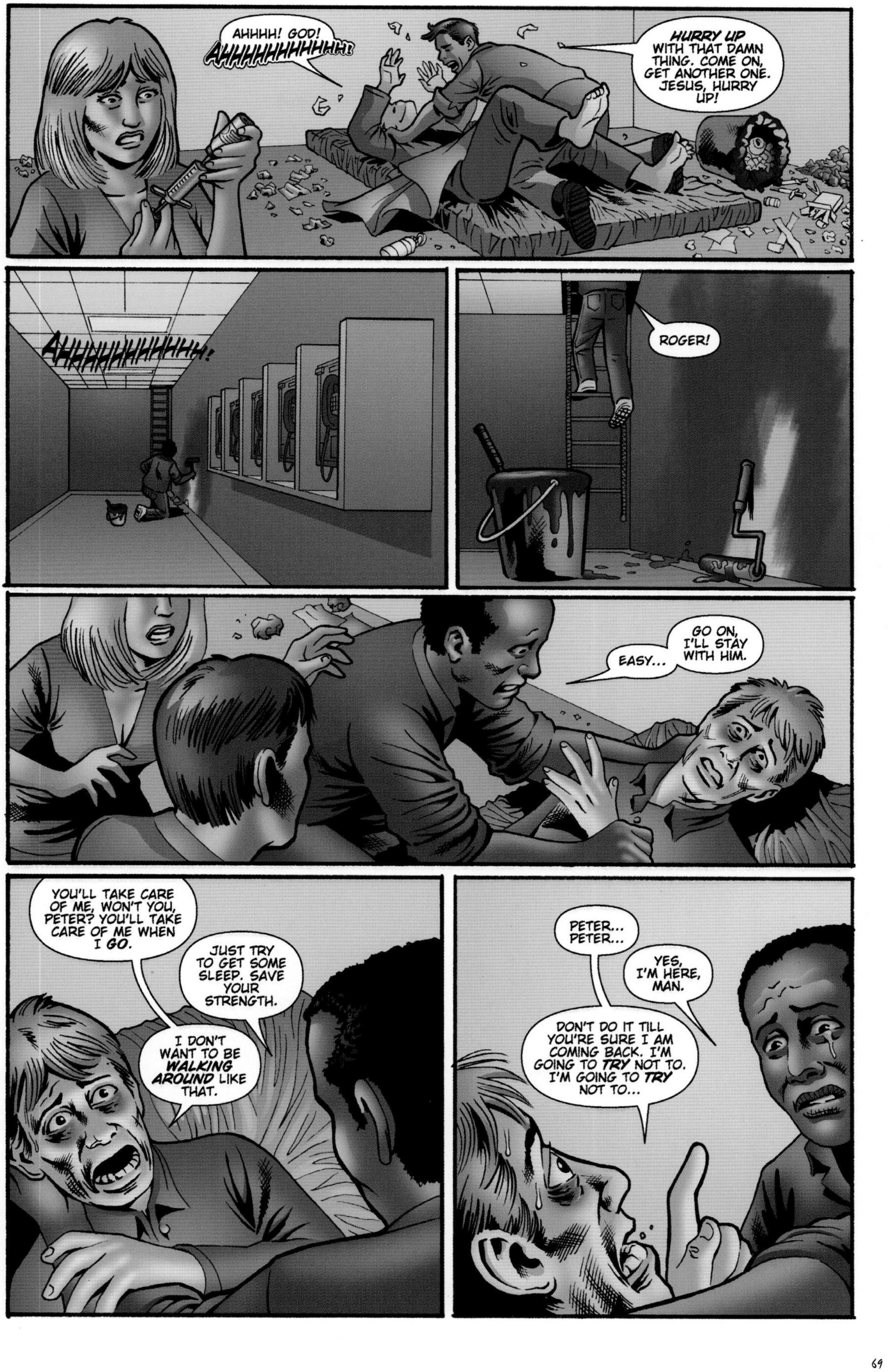
AHHHH! GOD!
AHHHHHHHHHH!
HURRY UP WITH THAT DAMN THING. COME ON, GET ANOTHER ONE. JESUS, HURRY UP!
AHHHHHHHHHHH!
ROGER!
EASY...
GO ON, I'LL STAY WITH HIM.
YOU'LL TAKE CARE OF ME, WON'T YOU, PETER? YOU'LL TAKE CARE OF ME WHEN I GO.
JUST TRY TO GET SOME SLEEP. SAVE YOUR STRENGTH.
I DON'T WANT TO BE WALKING AROUND LIKE THAT.
PETER... PETER...
YES, I'M HERE, MAN.
DON'T DO IT TILL YOU'RE SURE I AM COMING BACK. I'M GOING TO TRY NOT TO. I'M GOING TO TRY NOT TO...

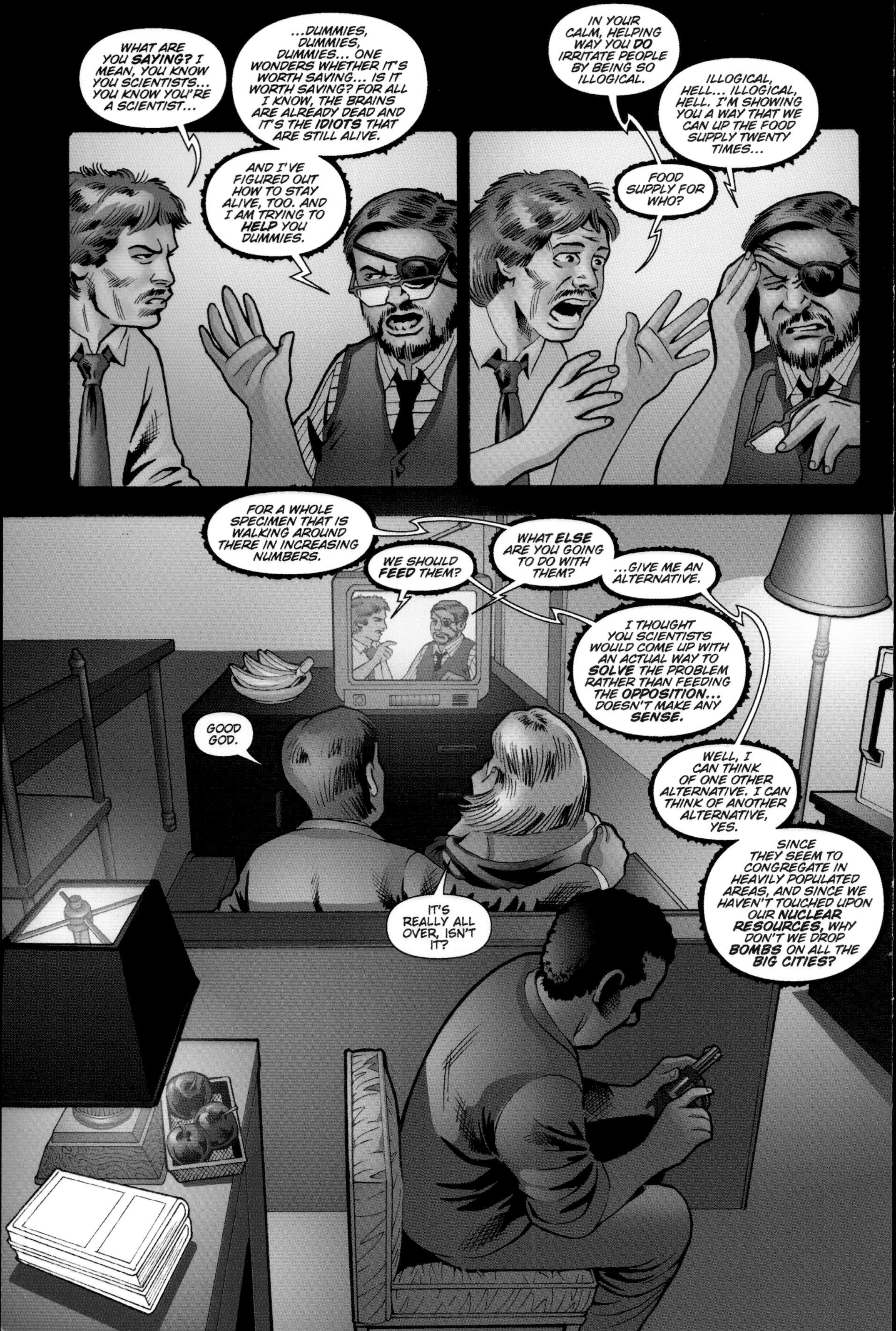
WHAT ARE YOU SAYING? I MEAN, YOU KNOW YOU SCIENTISTS... YOU KNOW YOU'RE A SCIENTIST...
...DUMMIES, DUMMIES, DUMMIES... ONE WONDERS WHETHER IT'S WORTH SAVING... IS IT WORTH SAVING? FOR ALL I KNOW, THE BRAINS ARE ALREADY DEAD AND IT'S THE IDIOTS THAT ARE STILL ALIVE.
AND I'VE FIGURED OUT HOW TO STAY ALIVE, TOO. AND I AM TRYING TO HELP YOU DUMMIES.
IN YOUR CALM, HELPING WAY YOU DO IRRITATE PEOPLE BY BEING SO ILLOGICAL.
ILLOGICAL, HELL... ILLOGICAL, HELL. I'M SHOWING YOU A WAY THAT WE CAN UP THE FOOD SUPPLY TWENTY TIMES...
FOOD SUPPLY FOR WHO?
FOR A WHOLE SPECIMEN THAT IS WALKING AROUND THERE IN INCREASING NUMBERS.
WE SHOULD FEED THEM?
WHAT ELSE ARE YOU GOING TO DO WITH THEM?
...GIVE ME AN ALTERNATIVE.
I THOUGHT YOU SCIENTISTS WOULD COME UP WITH AN ACTUAL WAY TO SOLVE THE PROBLEM RATHER THAN FEEDING THE OPPOSITION... DOESN'T MAKE ANY SENSE.
GOOD GOD.
WELL, I CAN THINK OF ONE OTHER ALTERNATIVE. I CAN THINK OF ANOTHER ALTERNATIVE, YES.
SINCE THEY SEEM TO CONGREGATE IN HEAVILY POPULATED AREAS, AND SINCE WE HAVEN'T TOUCHED UPON OUR NUCLEAR RESOURCES, WHY DON'T WE DROP BOMBS ON ALL THE BIG CITIES?
IT'S REALLY ALL OVER, ISN'T IT?

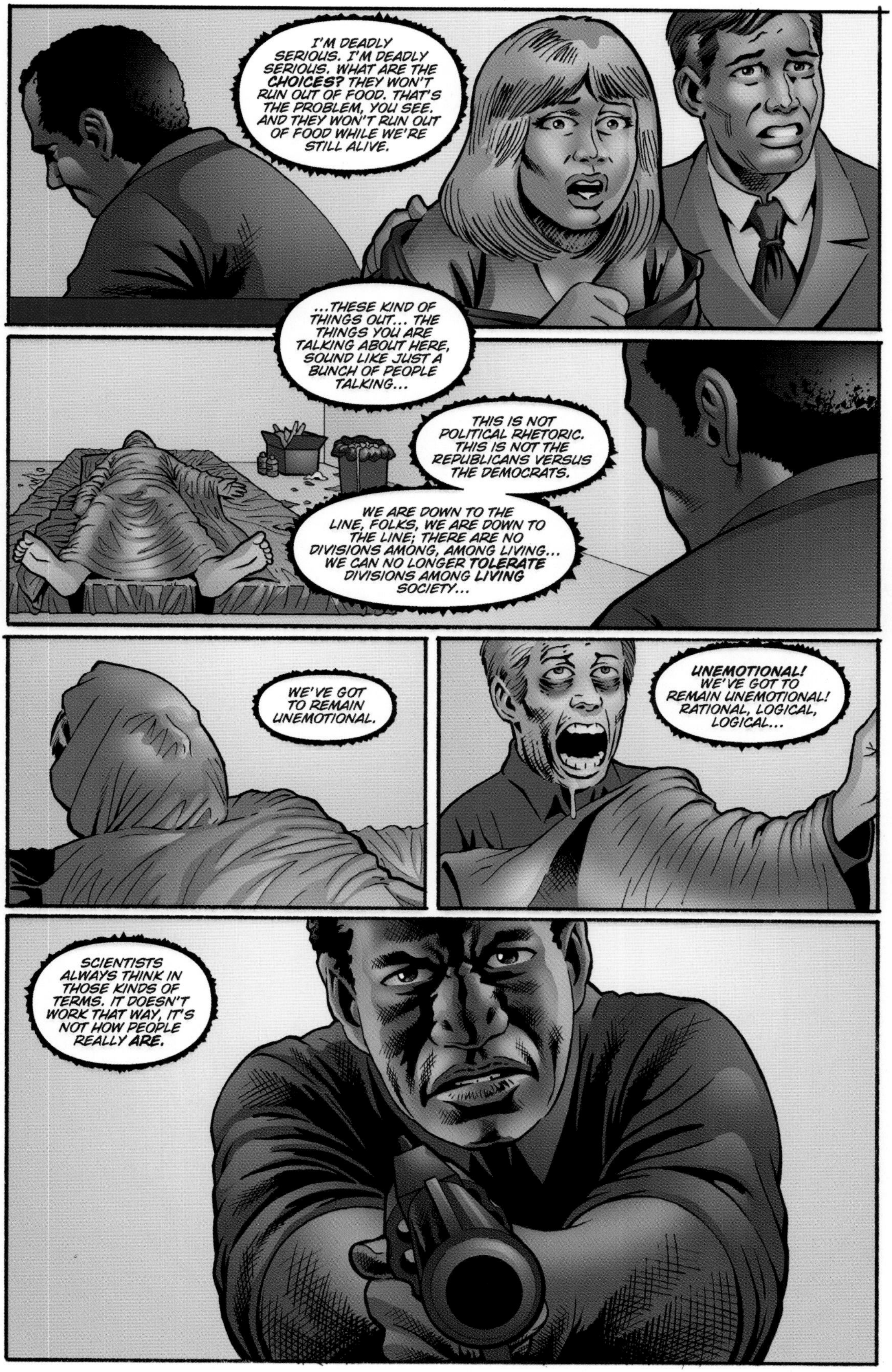
I'M DEADLY SERIOUS. I'M DEADLY SERIOUS. WHAT ARE THE CHOICES? THEY WON'T RUN OUT OF FOOD. THAT'S THE PROBLEM, YOU SEE. AND THEY WON'T RUN OUT OF FOOD WHILE WE'RE STILL ALIVE.
...THESE KIND OF THINGS OUT... THE THINGS YOU ARE TALKING ABOUT HERE, SOUND LIKE JUST A BUNCH OF PEOPLE TALKING...
THIS IS NOT POLITICAL RHETORIC. THIS IS NOT THE REPUBLICANS VERSUS THE DEMOCRATS.
WE ARE DOWN TO THE LINE, FOLKS, WE ARE DOWN TO THE LINE; THERE ARE NO DIVISIONS AMONG, AMONG LIVING... WE CAN NO LONGER TOLERATE DIVISIONS AMONG LIVING SOCIETY...
WE'VE GOT TO REMAIN UNEMOTIONAL.
UNEMOTIONAL! WE'VE GOT TO REMAIN UNEMOTIONAL! RATIONAL, LOGICAL, LOGICAL...
SCIENTISTS ALWAYS THINK IN THOSE KINDS OF TERMS. IT DOESN'T WORK THAT WAY, IT'S NOT HOW PEOPLE REALLY ARE.

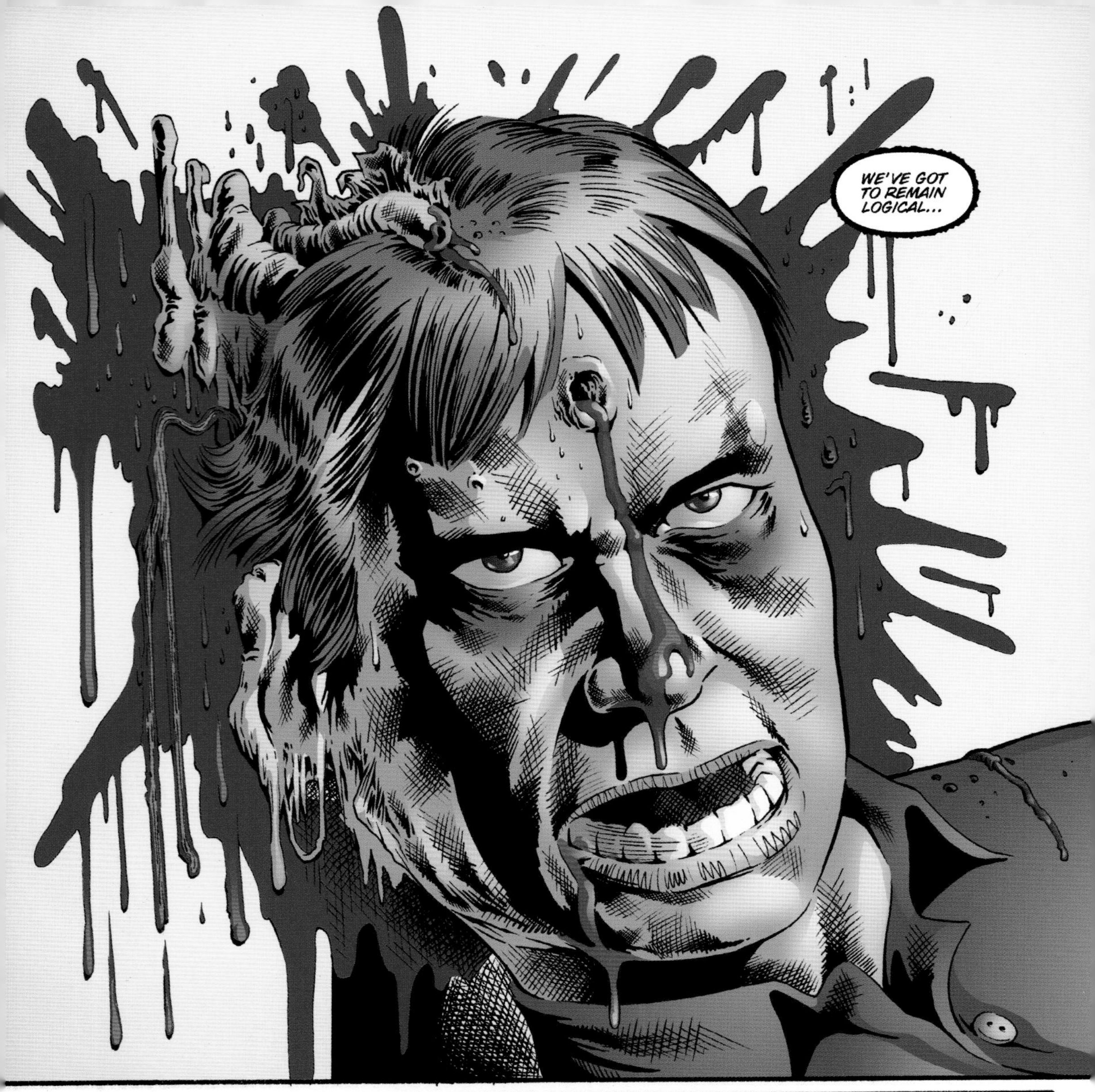
WE'VE GOT TO REMAIN LOGICAL...

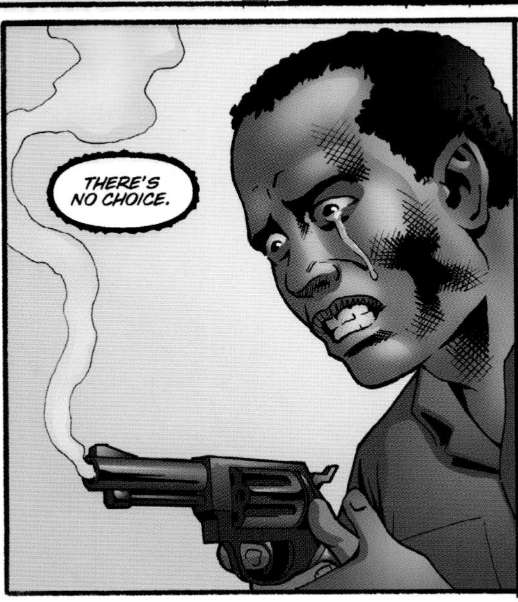
THERE'S NO CHOICE.

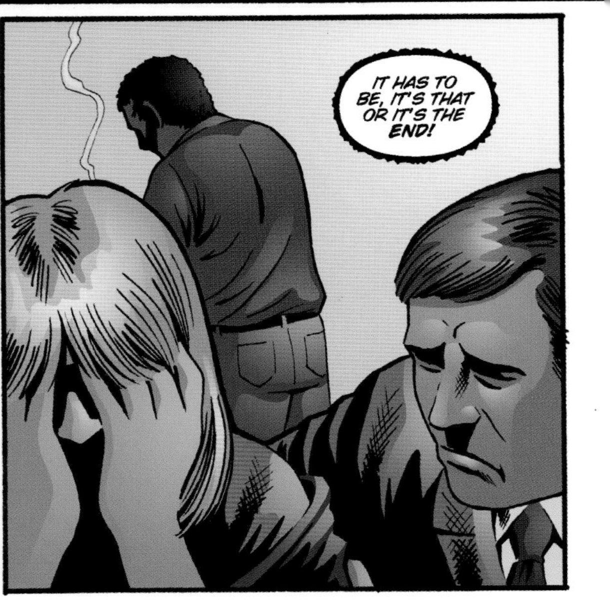
IT HAS TO BE, IT'S THAT OR IT'S THE END!

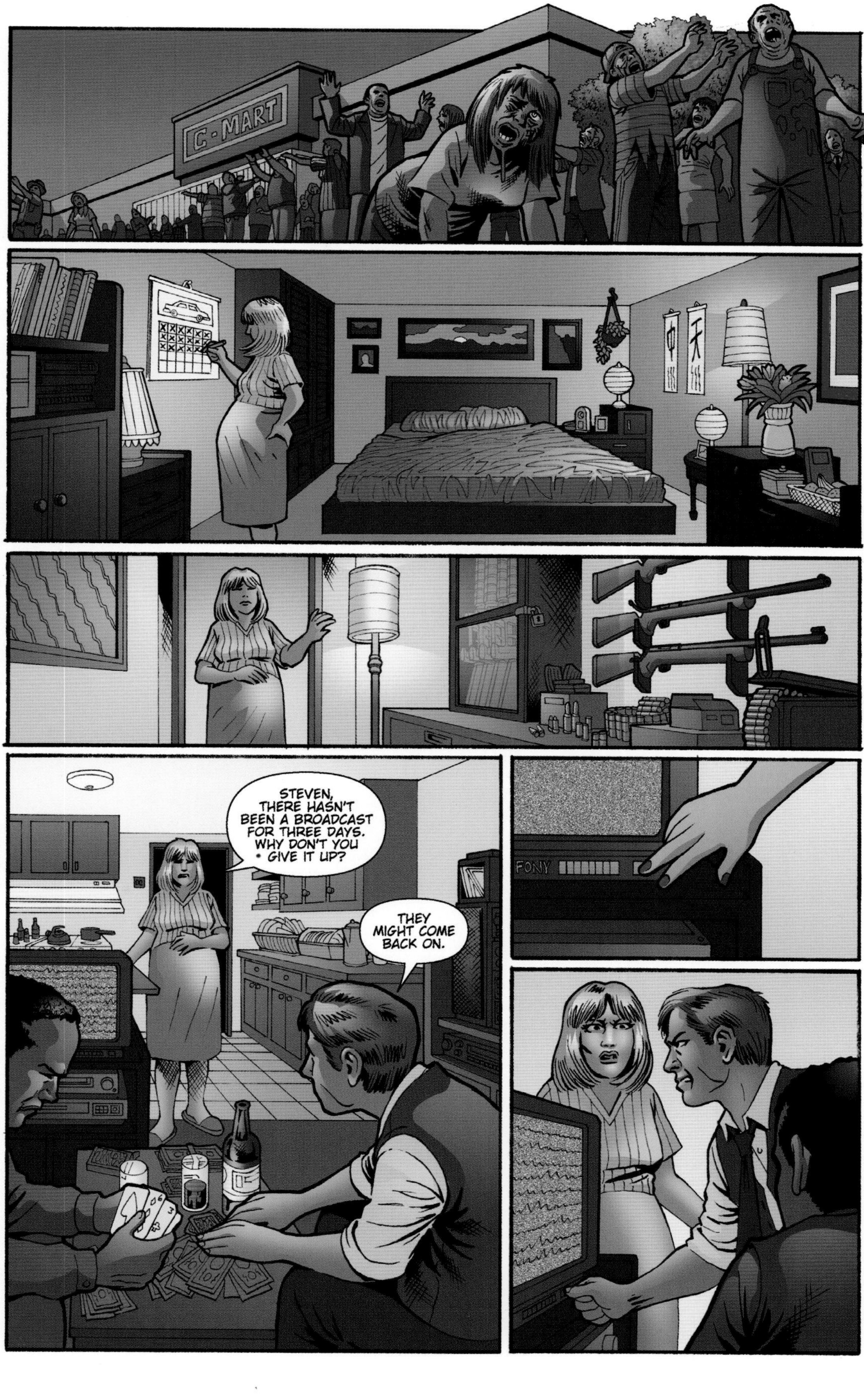
C-MART
STEVEN, THERE HASN'T BEEN A BROADCAST FOR THREE DAYS. WHY DON'T YOU GIVE IT UP?
THEY MIGHT COME BACK ON.
FONY

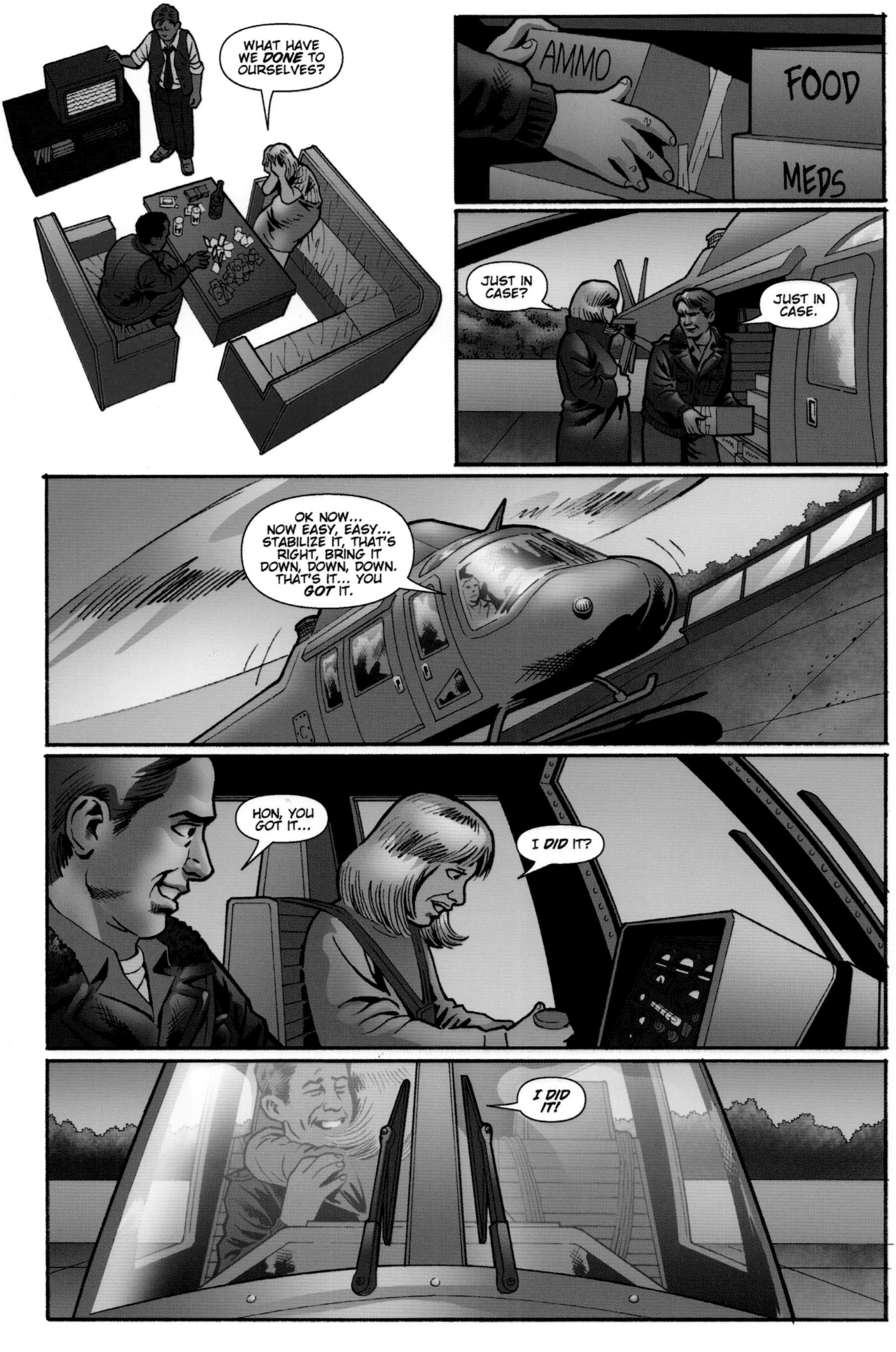
WHAT HAVE WE DONE TO OURSELVES?
AMMO
FOOD
MEDS
JUST IN CASE?
JUST IN CASE.
OK NOW... NOW EASY, EASY... STABILIZE IT, THAT'S RIGHT, BRING IT DOWN, DOWN, DOWN. THAT'S IT... YOU GOT IT.
HON, YOU GOT IT...
I DID IT?
I DID IT!

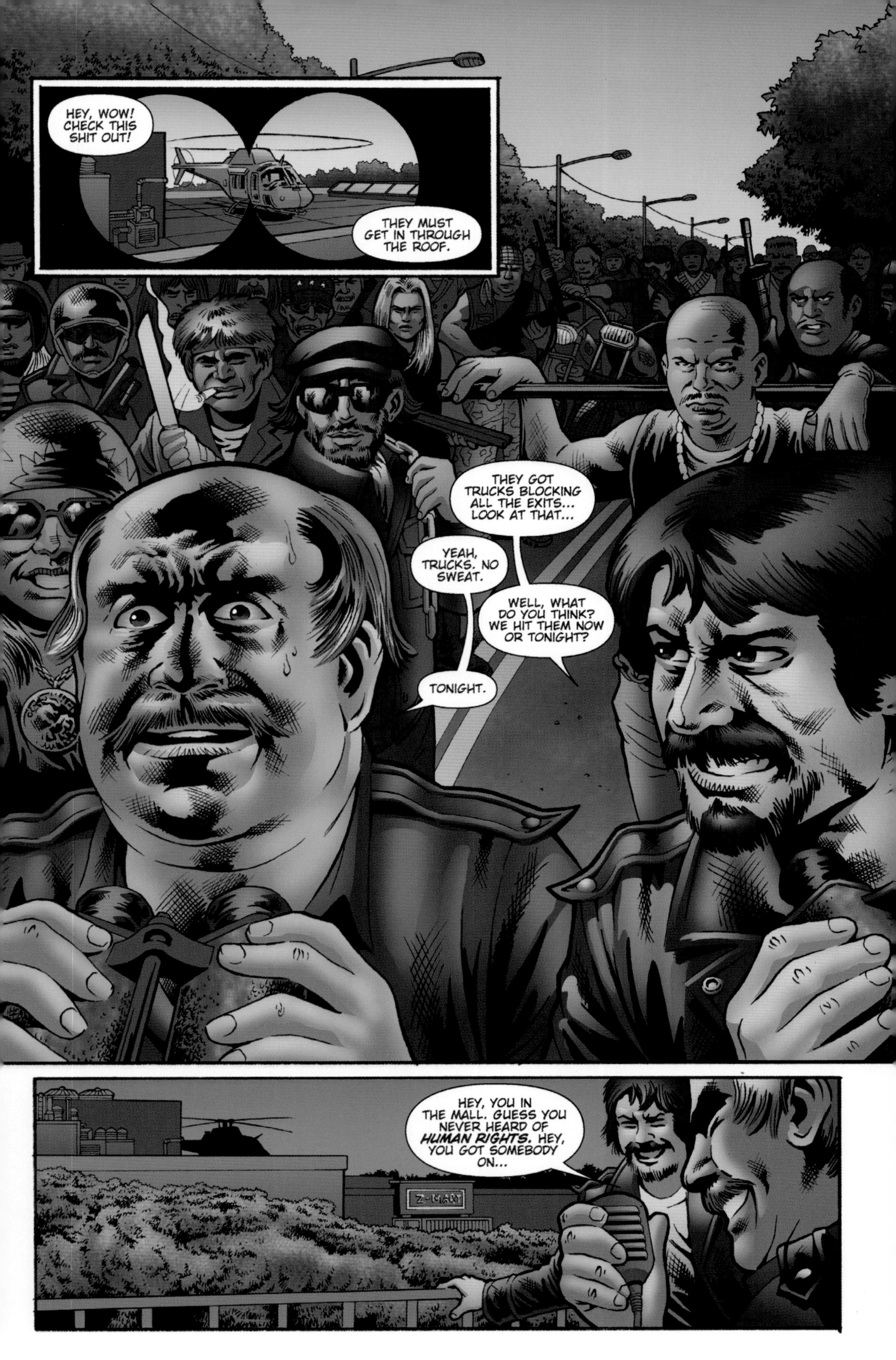
HEY, WOW! CHECK THIS SHIT OUT!
THEY MUST GET IN THROUGH THE ROOF.
THEY GOT TRUCKS BLOCKING ALL THE EXITS... LOOK AT THAT...
YEAH, TRUCKS. NO SWEAT.
WELL, WHAT DO YOU THINK? WE HIT THEM NOW OR TONIGHT?
TONIGHT.
HEY, YOU IN THE MALL. GUESS YOU NEVER HEARD OF ***HUMAN RIGHTS.*** HEY, YOU GOT SOMEBODY ON...
Z-MART

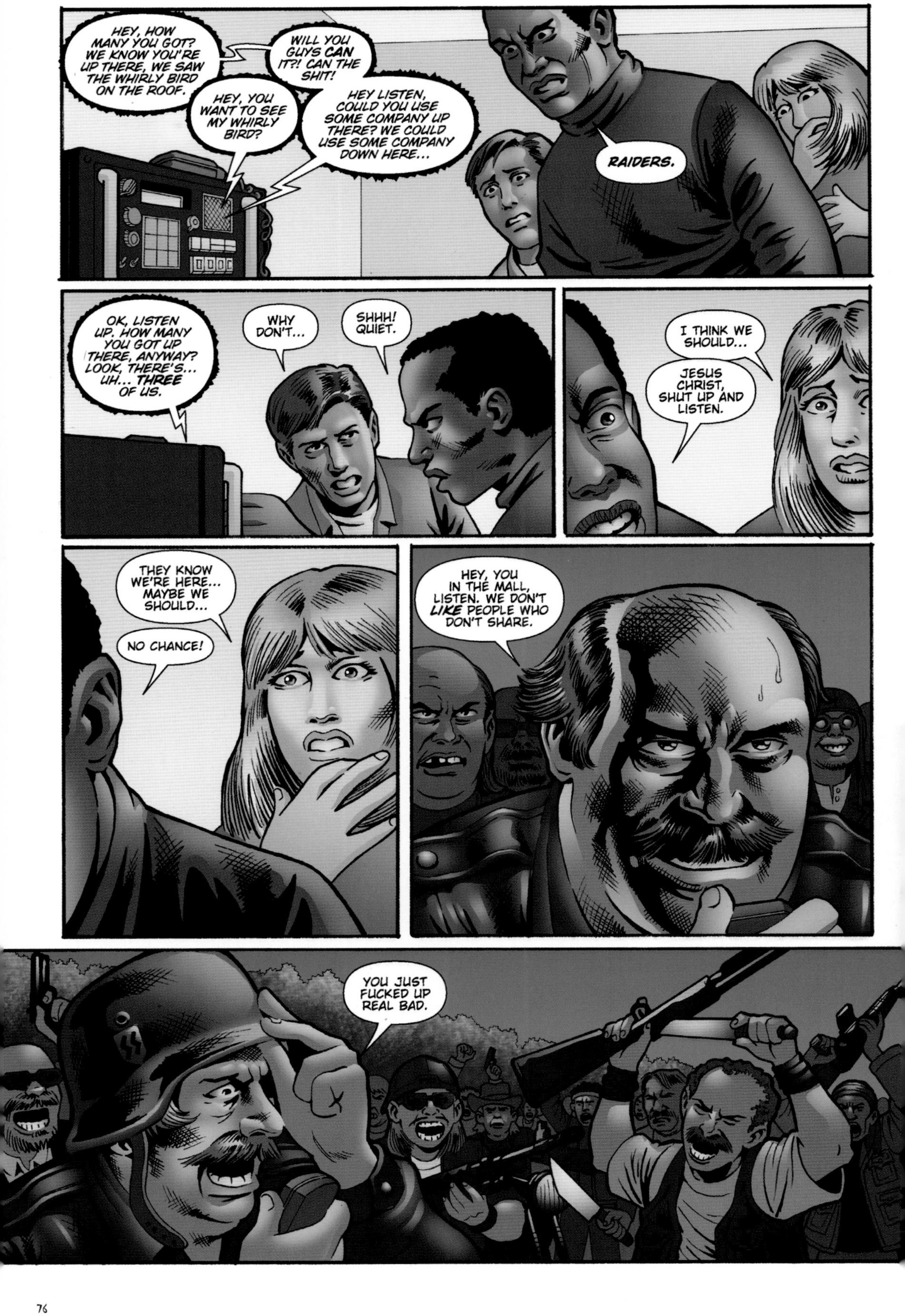
HEY, HOW MANY YOU GOT? WE KNOW YOU'RE UP THERE, WE SAW THE WHIRLY BIRD ON THE ROOF.
WILL YOU GUYS CAN IT?! CAN THE SHIT!
HEY, YOU WANT TO SEE MY WHIRLY BIRD?
HEY LISTEN, COULD YOU USE SOME COMPANY UP THERE? WE COULD USE SOME COMPANY DOWN HERE...
RAIDERS.
OK, LISTEN UP. HOW MANY YOU GOT UP THERE, ANYWAY? LOOK, THERE'S... UH... THREE OF US.
WHY DON'T...
SHHH! QUIET.
I THINK WE SHOULD...
JESUS CHRIST, SHUT UP AND LISTEN.
THEY KNOW WE'RE HERE... MAYBE WE SHOULD...
NO CHANCE!
HEY, YOU IN THE MALL, LISTEN. WE DON'T LIKE PEOPLE WHO DON'T SHARE.
YOU JUST FUCKED UP REAL BAD.

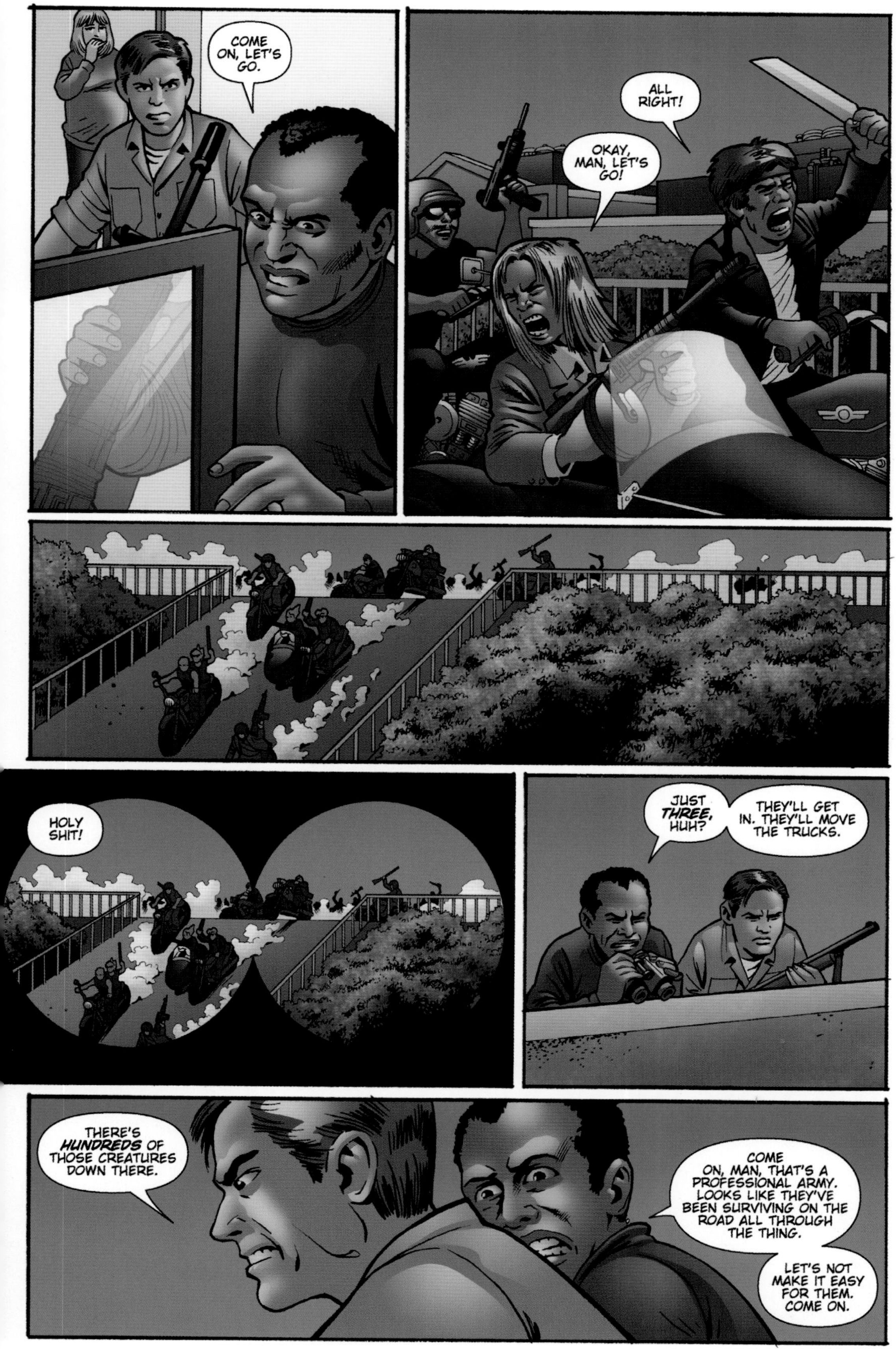
COME ON, LET'S GO.
ALL RIGHT!
OKAY, MAN, LET'S GO!
HOLY SHIT!
JUST THREE, HUH?
THEY'LL GET IN. THEY'LL MOVE THE TRUCKS.
THERE'S HUNDREDS OF THOSE CREATURES DOWN THERE.
COME ON, MAN, THAT'S A PROFESSIONAL ARMY. LOOKS LIKE THEY'VE BEEN SURVIVING ON THE ROAD ALL THROUGH THE THING.
LET'S NOT MAKE IT EASY FOR THEM. COME ON.

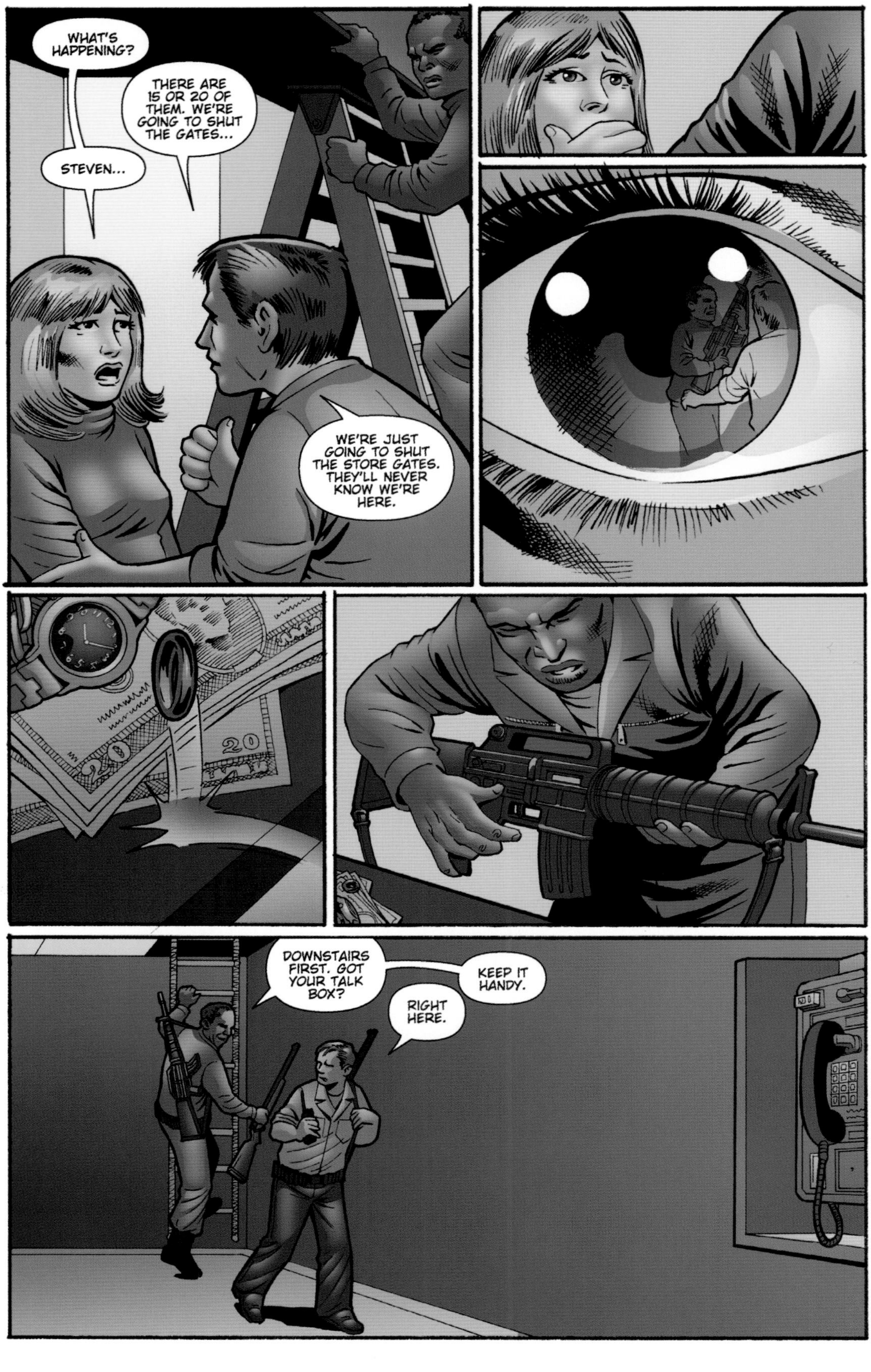
WHAT'S HAPPENING?
STEVEN...
THERE ARE 15 OR 20 OF THEM. WE'RE GOING TO SHUT THE GATES...
WE'RE JUST GOING TO SHUT THE STORE GATES. THEY'LL NEVER KNOW WE'RE HERE.
DOWNSTAIRS FIRST. GOT YOUR TALK BOX?
KEEP IT HANDY.
RIGHT HERE.

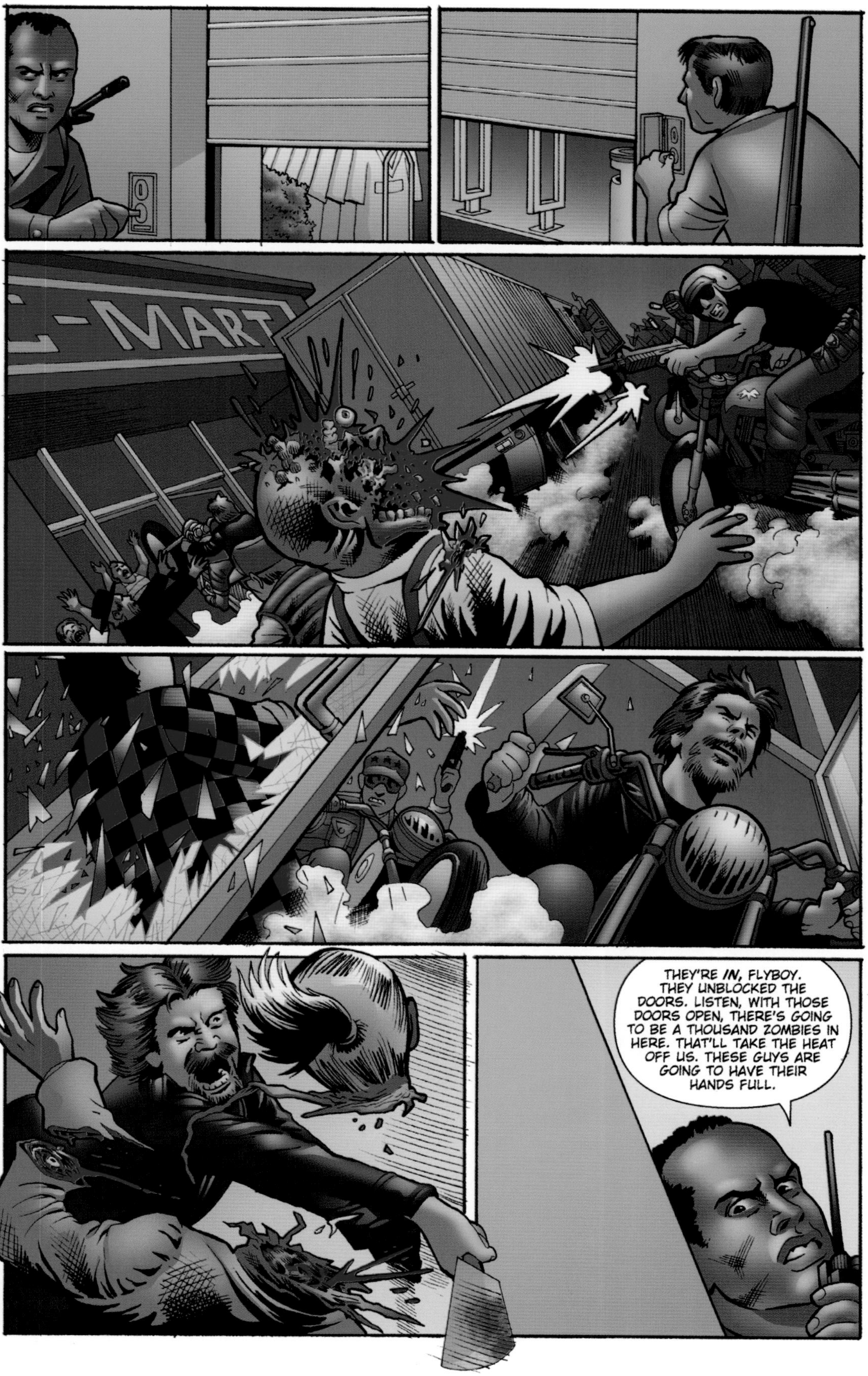
C-MART
THEY'RE IN, FLYBOY. THEY UNBLOCKED THE DOORS. LISTEN, WITH THOSE DOORS OPEN, THERE'S GOING TO BE A THOUSAND ZOMBIES IN HERE. THAT'LL TAKE THE HEAT OFF US. THESE GUYS ARE GOING TO HAVE THEIR HANDS FULL.

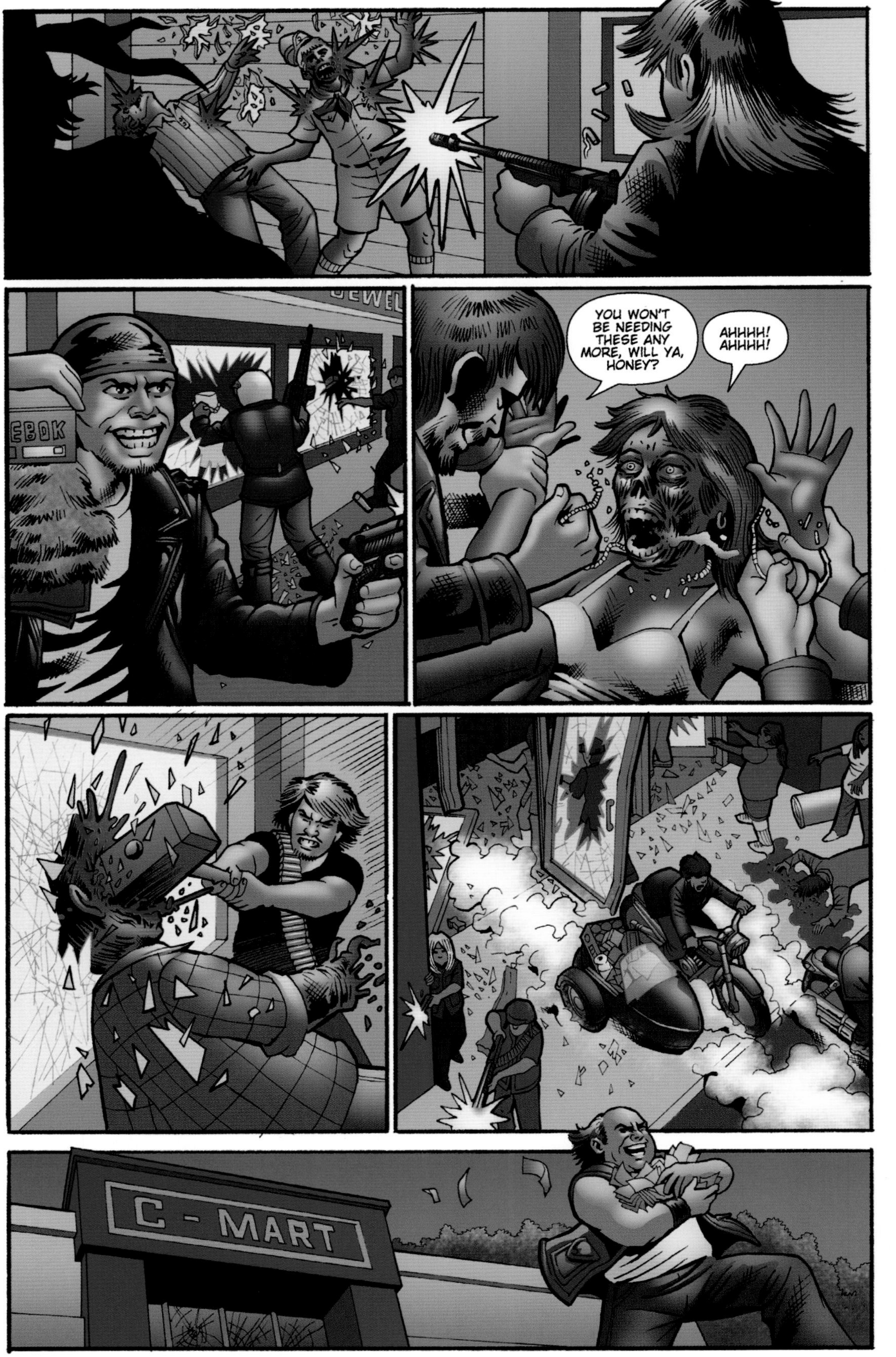
YOU WON'T BE NEEDING THESE ANY MORE, WILL YA, HONEY?
AHHHH! AHHHH!
C - MART

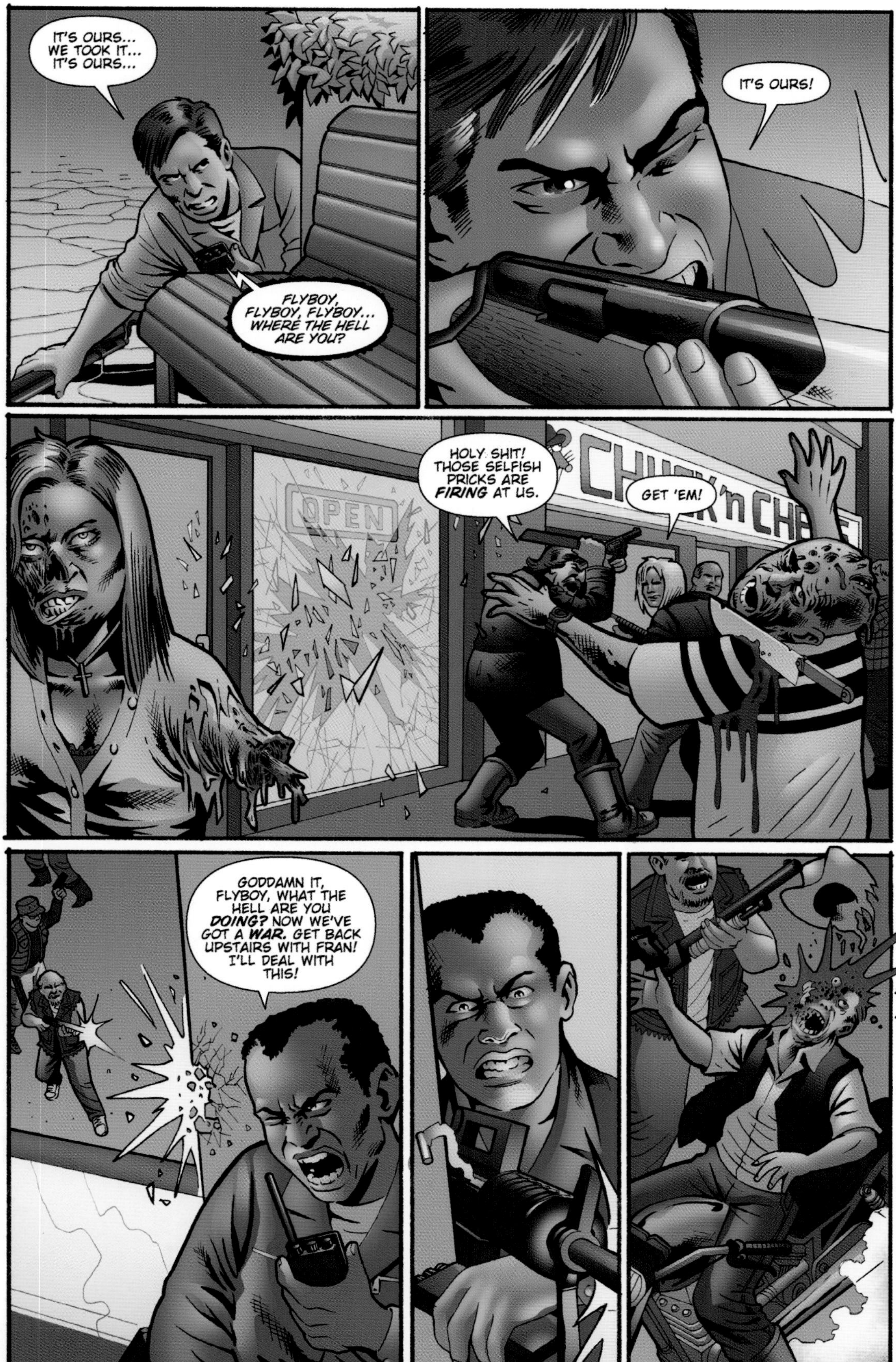
IT'S OURS... WE TOOK IT... IT'S OURS...
FLYBOY, FLYBOY, FLYBOY... WHERE THE HELL ARE YOU?
IT'S OURS!
HOLY SHIT! THOSE SELFISH PRICKS ARE FIRING AT US.
GET 'EM!
OPEN
GODDAMN IT, FLYBOY, WHAT THE HELL ARE YOU DOING? NOW WE'VE GOT A WAR. GET BACK UPSTAIRS WITH FRAN! I'LL DEAL WITH THIS!

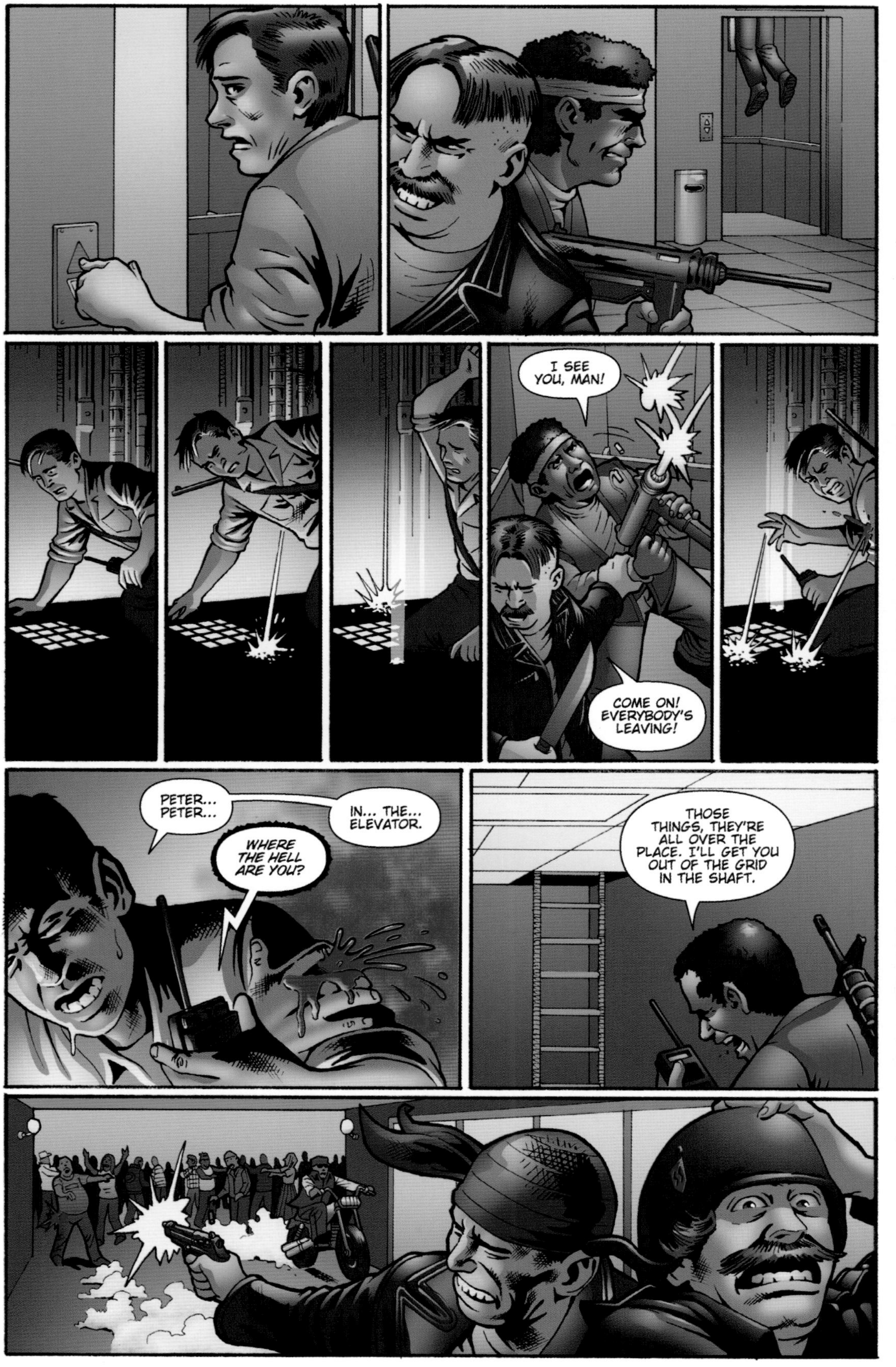
I SEE YOU, MAN!
COME ON! EVERYBODY'S LEAVING!
PETER... PETER...
IN... THE... ELEVATOR.
WHERE THE HELL ARE YOU?
THOSE THINGS, THEY'RE ALL OVER THE PLACE. I'LL GET YOU OUT OF THE GRID IN THE SHAFT.

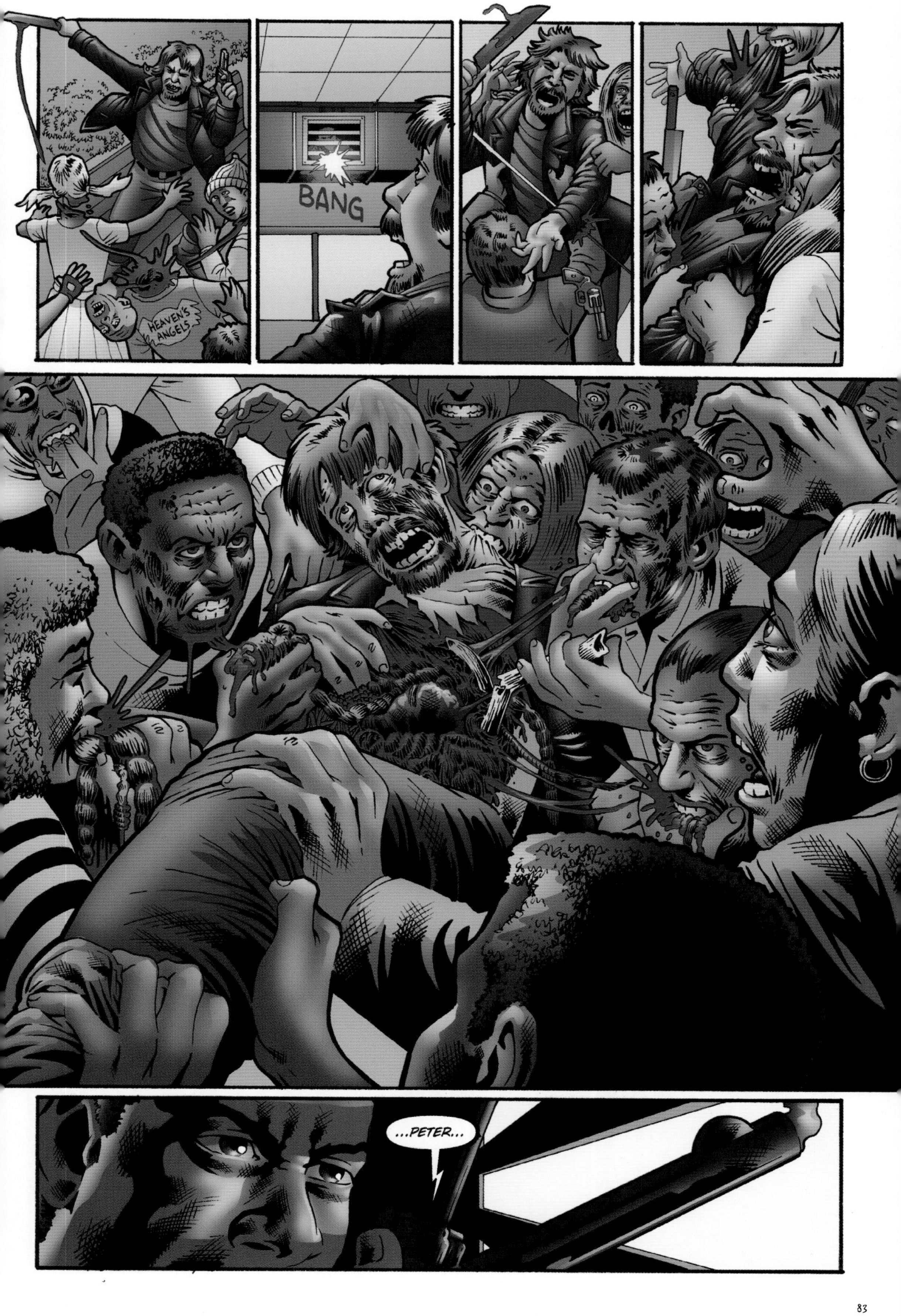
HEAVEN'S ANGELS
BANG
...PETER...

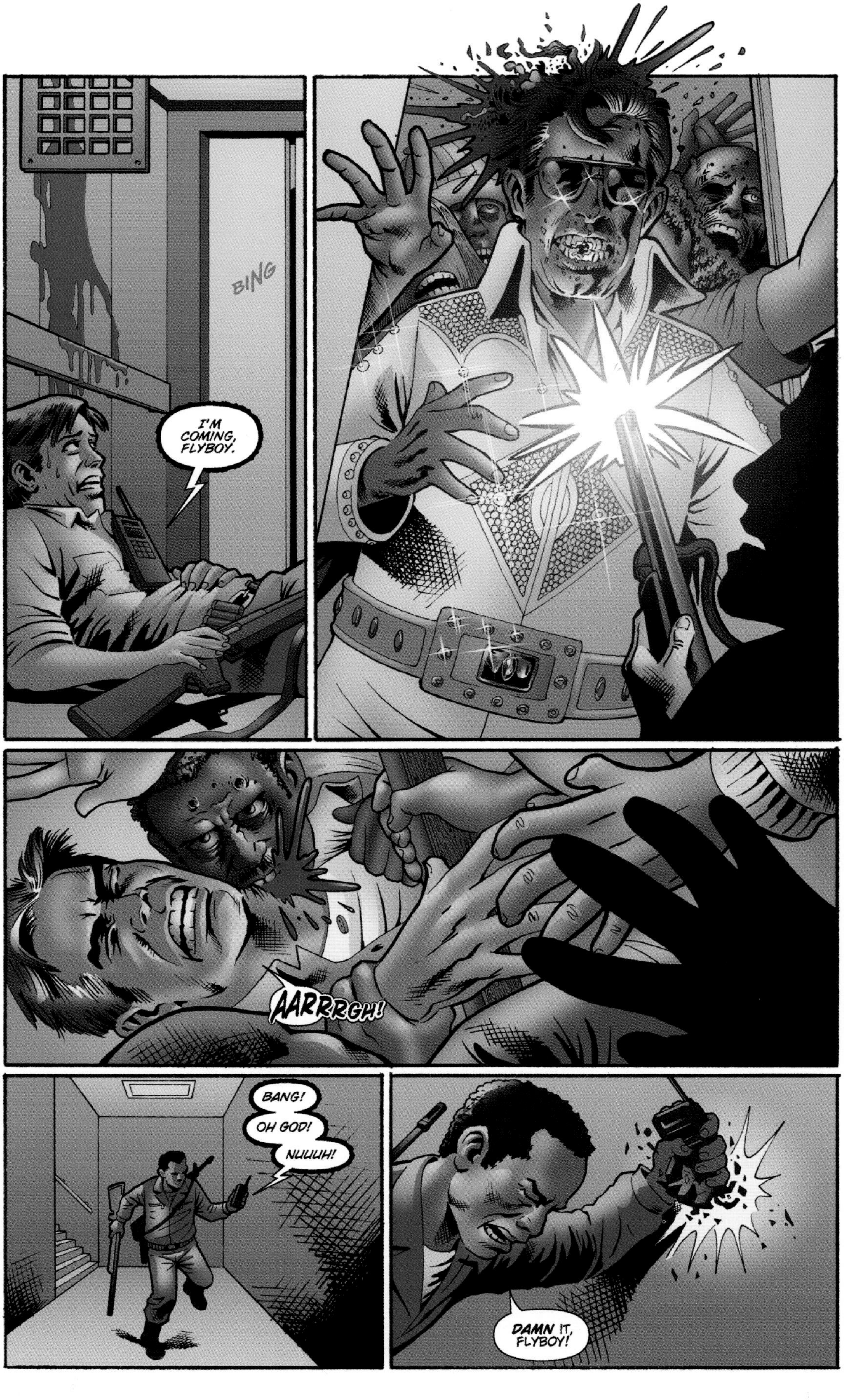
BING
I'M COMING, FLYBOY.
AARRRGH!
BANG!
OH GOD!
NUUUH!
DAMN IT, FLYBOY!

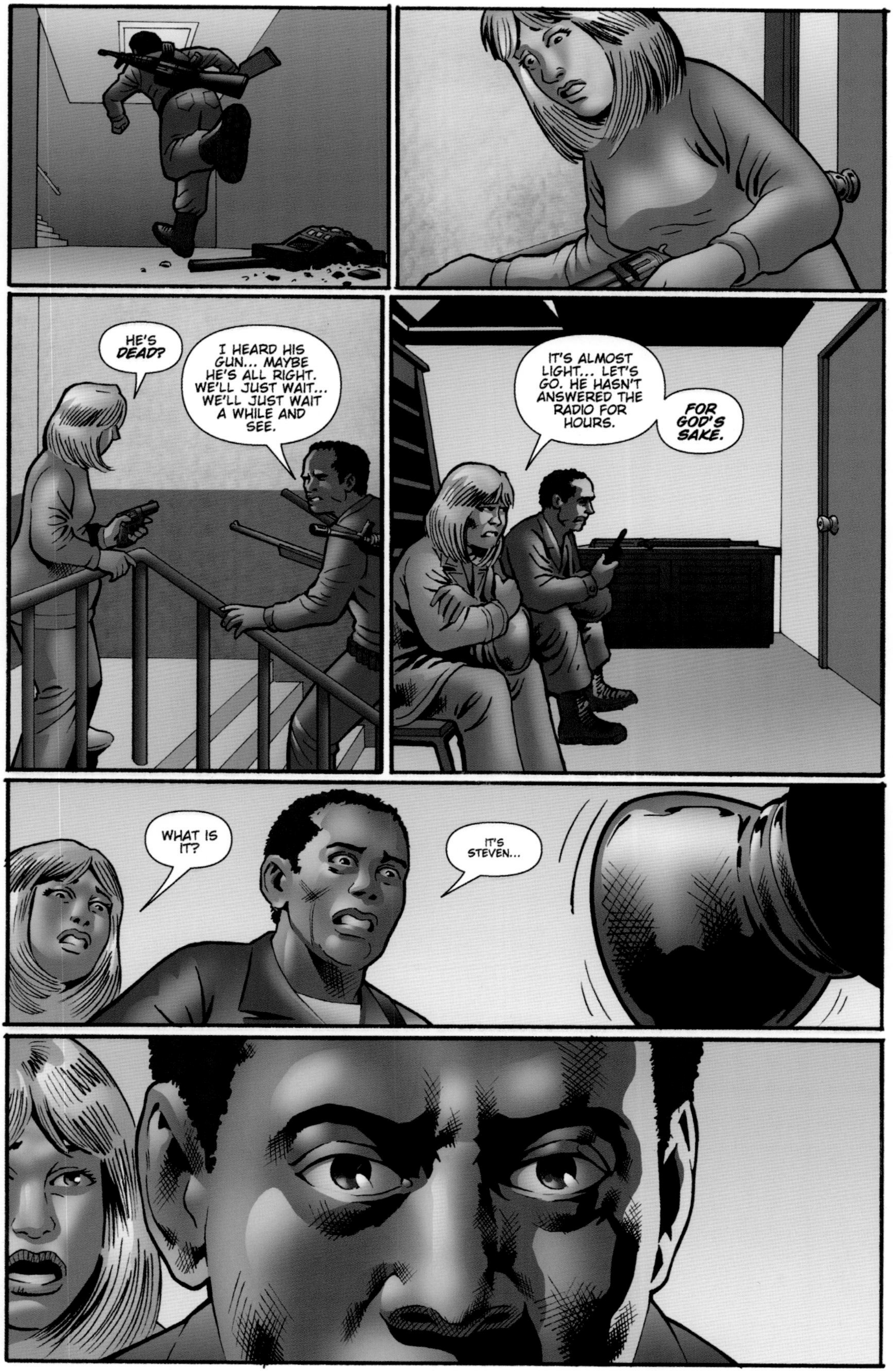
HE'S DEAD?
I HEARD HIS GUN... MAYBE HE'S ALL RIGHT. WE'LL JUST WAIT... WE'LL JUST WAIT A WHILE AND SEE.
IT'S ALMOST LIGHT... LET'S GO. HE HASN'T ANSWERED THE RADIO FOR HOURS.
FOR GOD'S SAKE.
WHAT IS IT?
IT'S STEVEN...

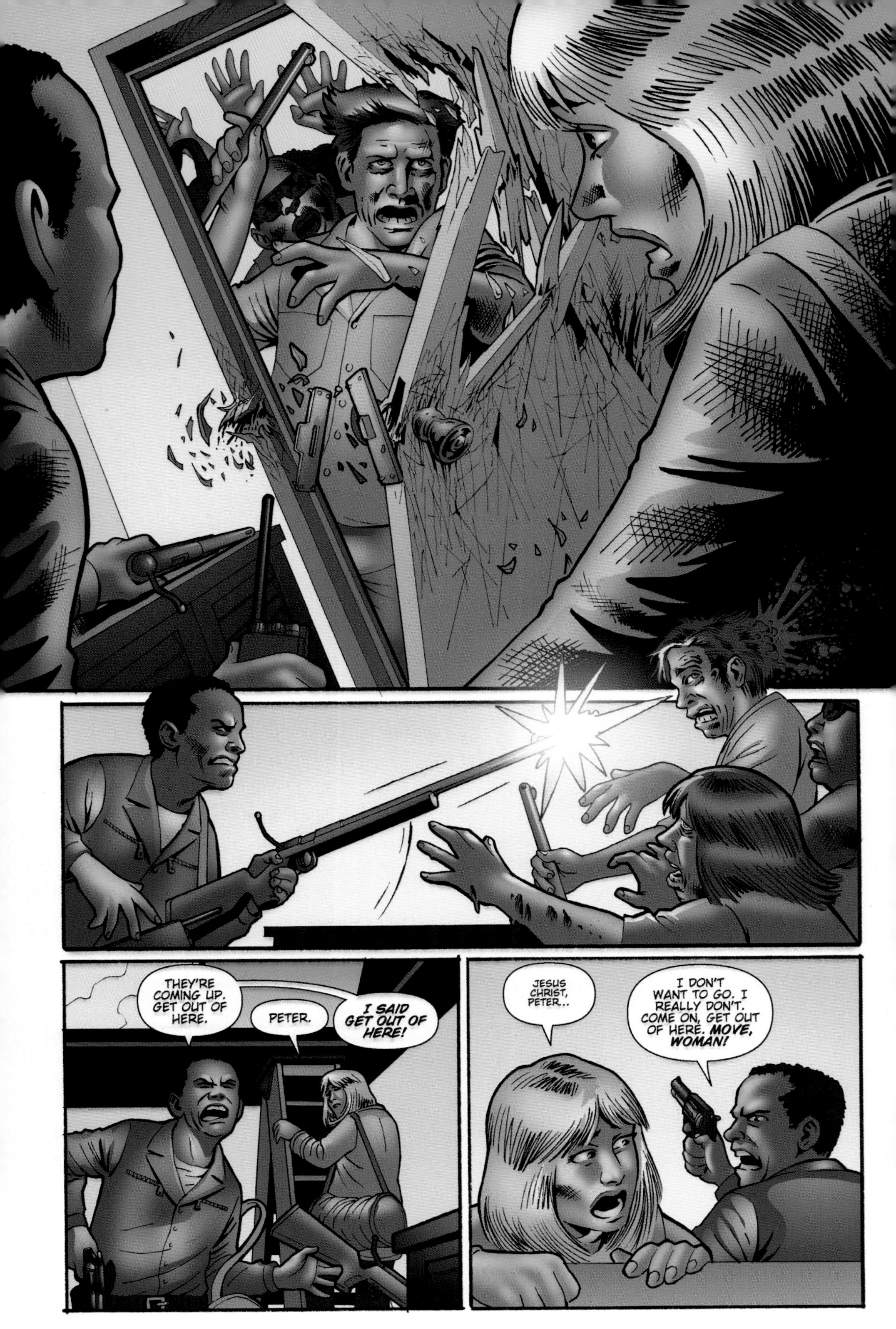
THEY'RE COMING UP. GET OUT OF HERE.
PETER.
I SAID GET OUT OF HERE!
JESUS CHRIST, PETER..
I DON'T WANT TO GO. I REALLY DON'T. COME ON, GET OUT OF HERE. MOVE, WOMAN!

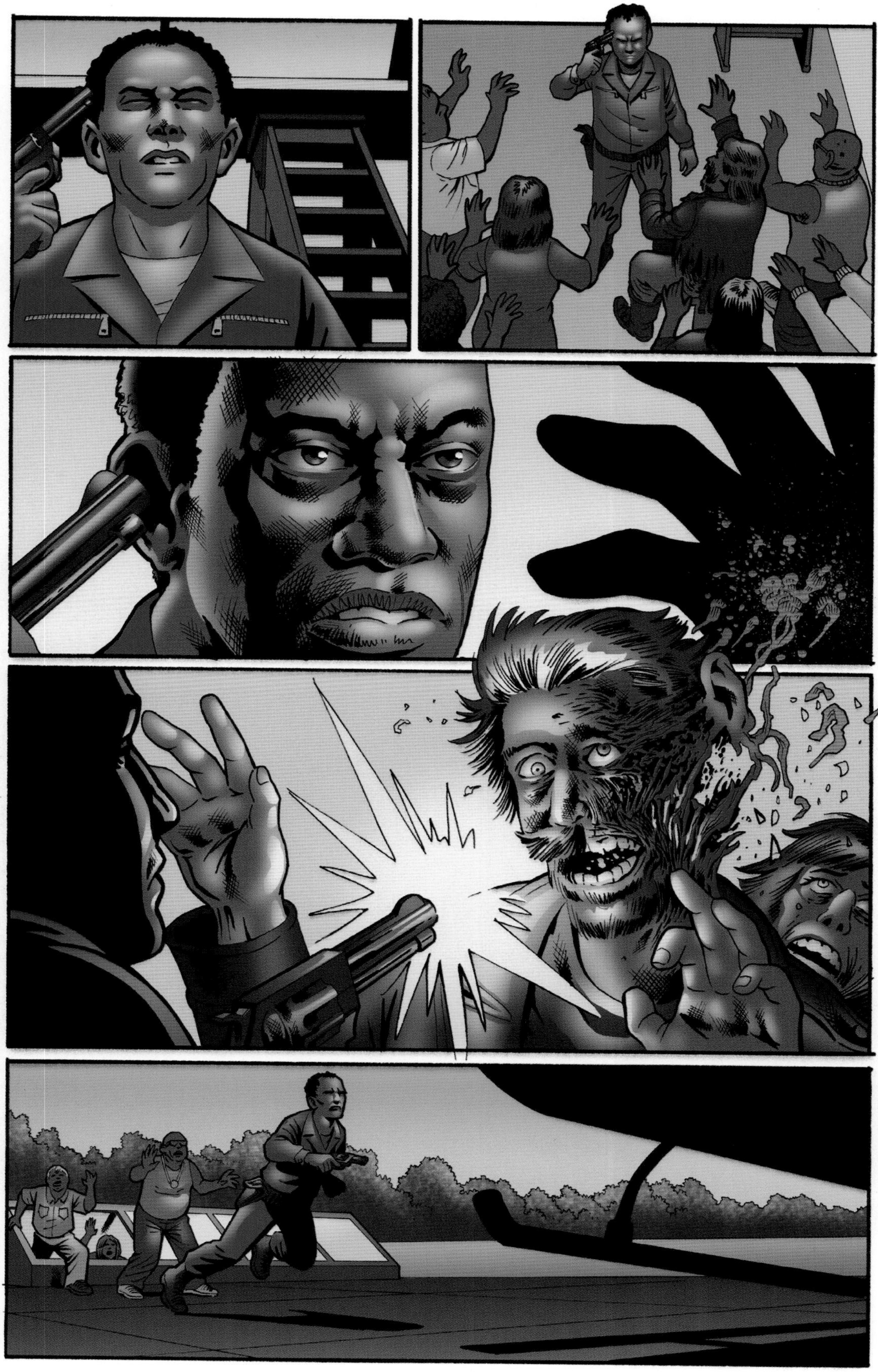

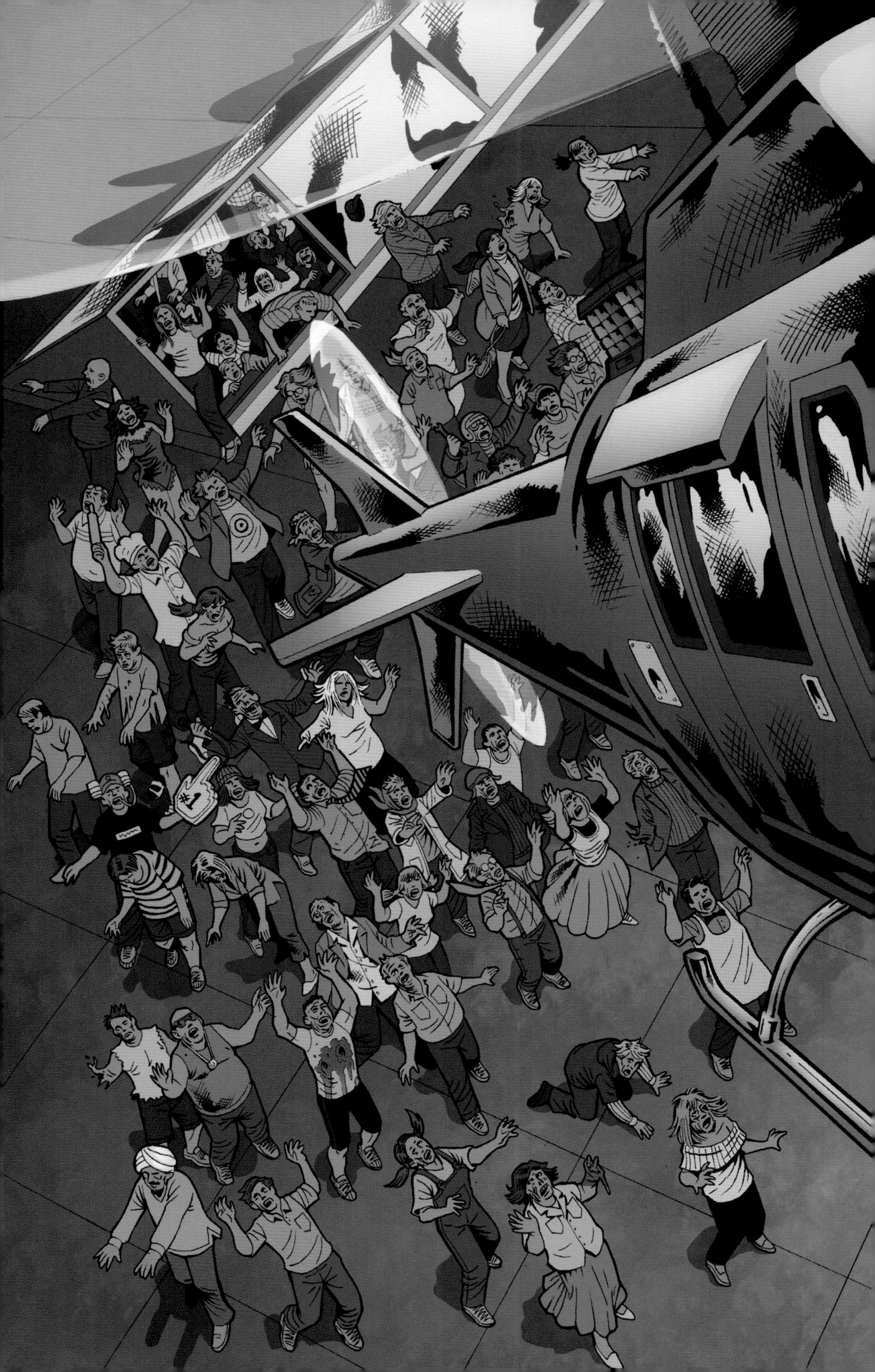
#1

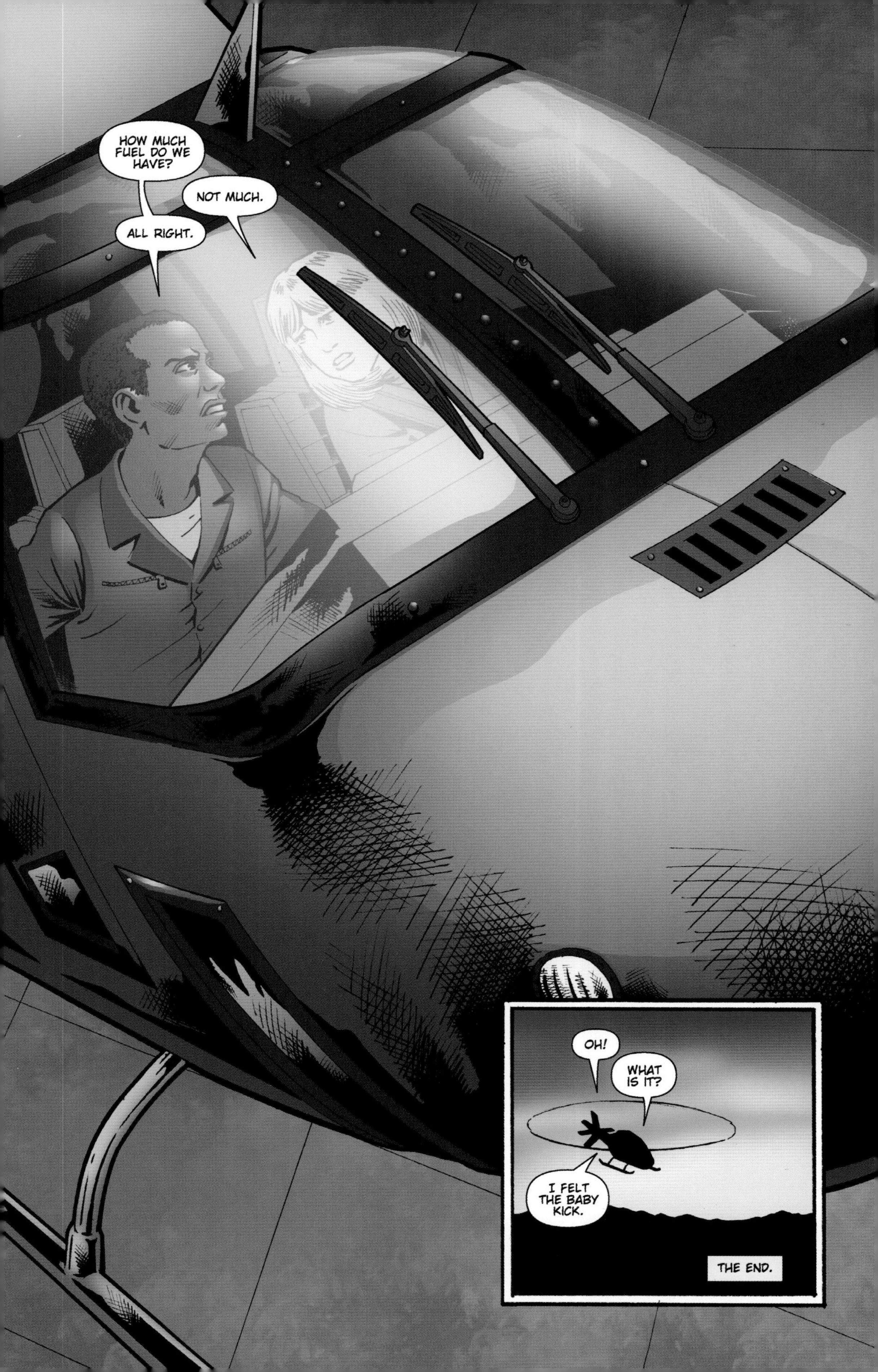
HOW MUCH FUEL DO WE HAVE?
NOT MUCH.
ALL RIGHT.
OH!
WHAT IS IT?
I FELT THE BABY KICK.
THE END.

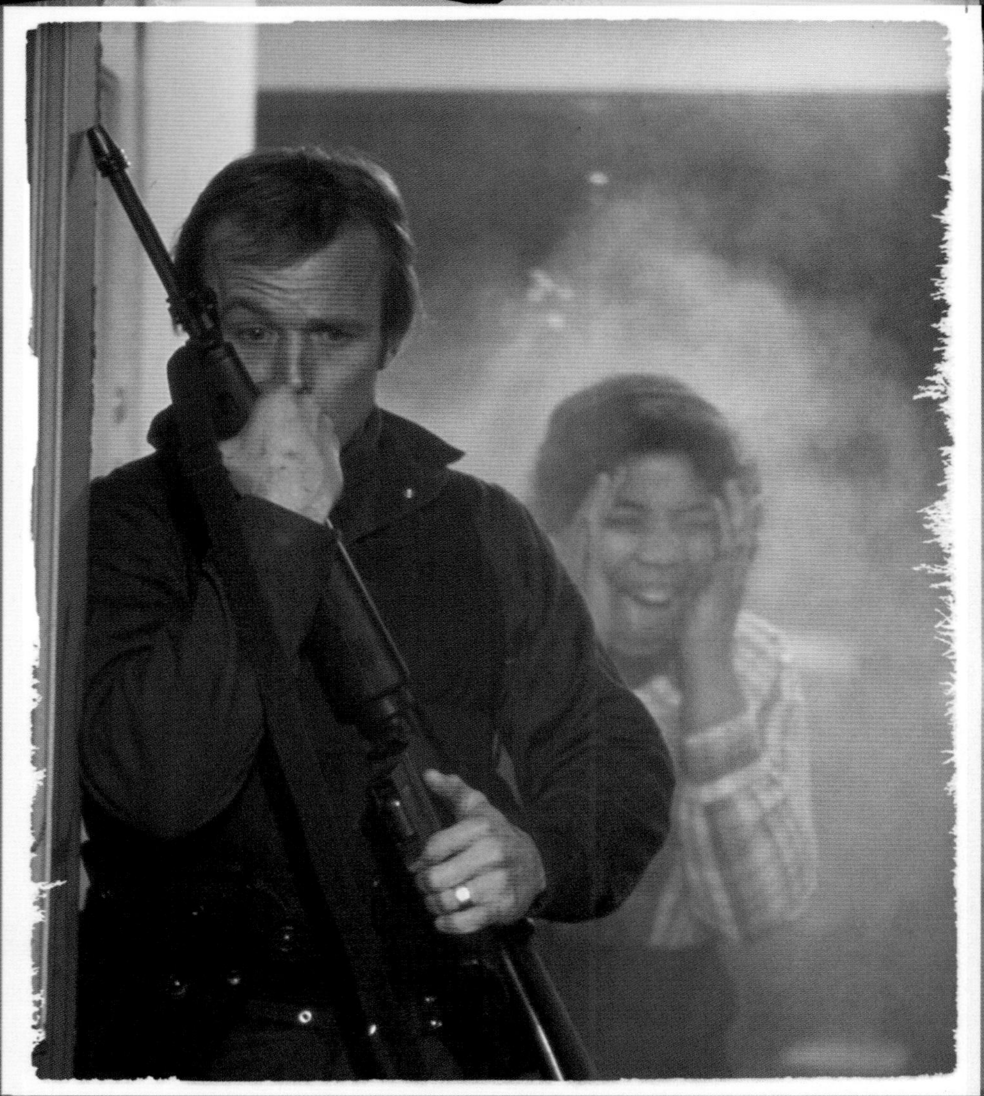

HERBERT R. STEINMANN AND BILLY BAXTER PRESENT A LAUREL GROUP PRODUCTION

IN ASSOCIATION WITH CLAUDIO ARGENTO & ALFREDO CUOMO

GEORGE A. ROMERO'S

DAWN OF THE DEAD

STARRING DAVID EMGE KEN FOREE SCOTT H. REINIGER GAYLEN ROSS

DIRECTOR OF PHOTOGRAPHY MICHAEL GORNICK

MUSIC BY THE GOBLINS WITH DARIO ARGENTO PRODUCED BY RICHARD P. RUBINSTEIN

WRITTEN AND DIRECTED BY GEORGE A. ROMERO

COLOR/127 MINS./NOT RATED

Photos by KATHERINE S. KOLBERT

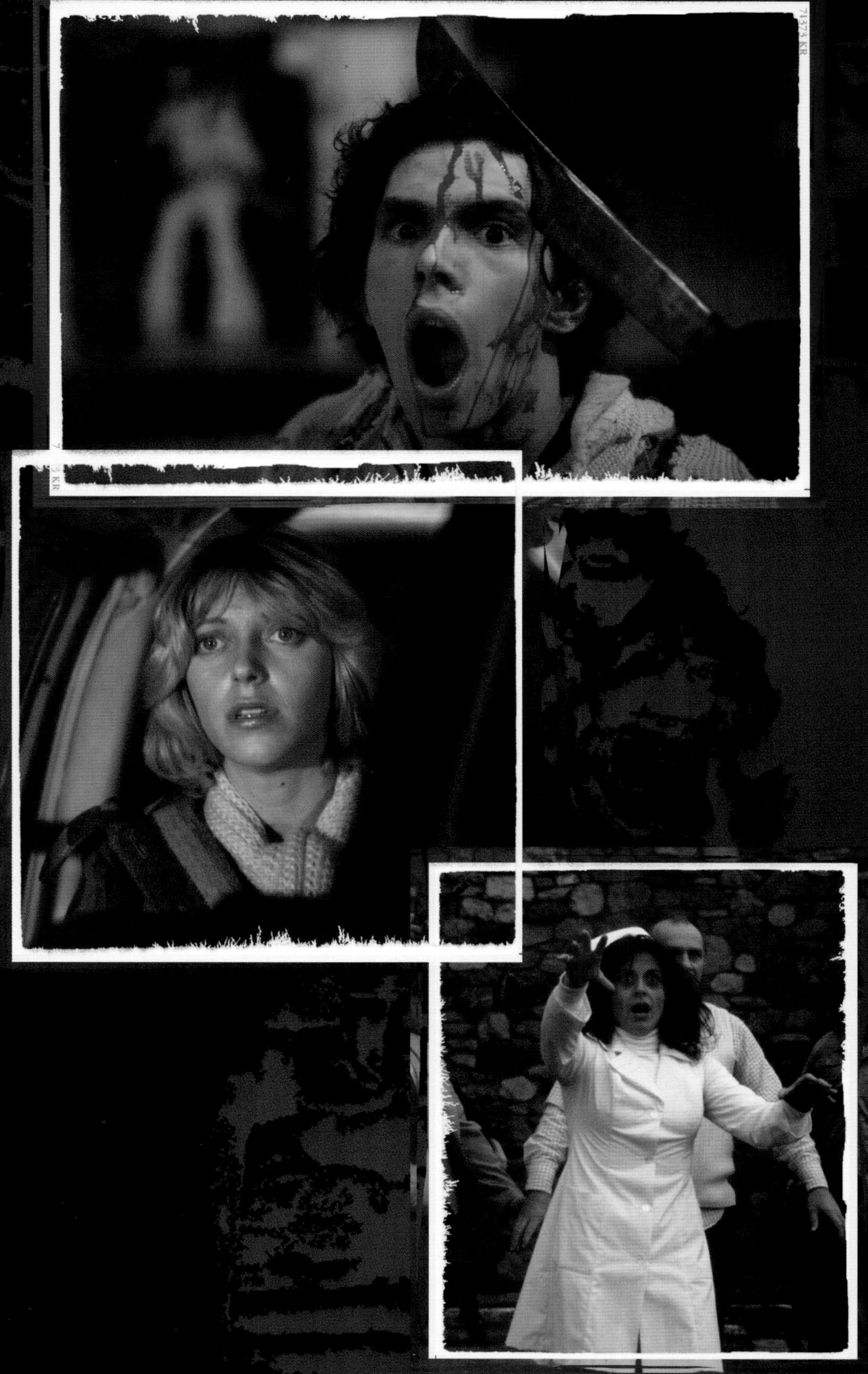
71373 KR

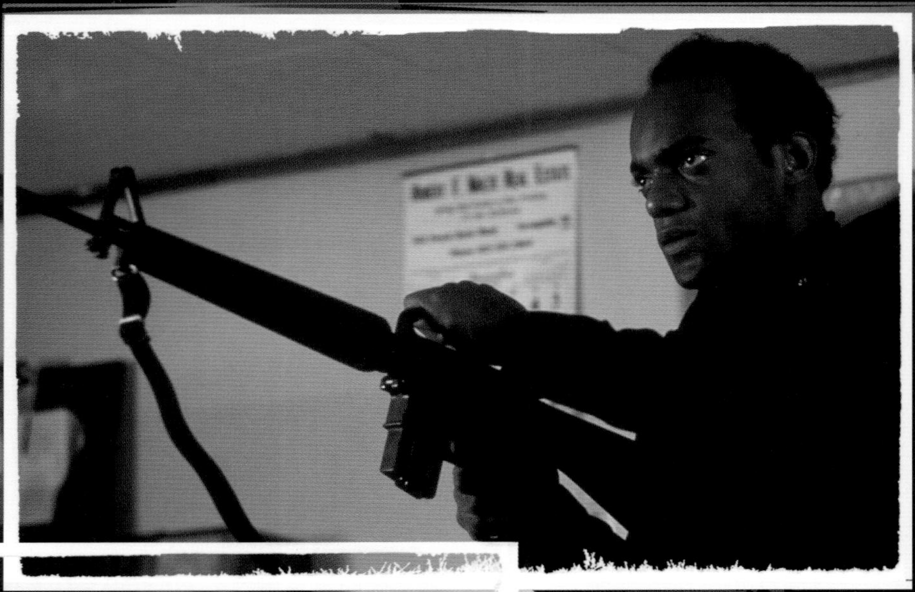

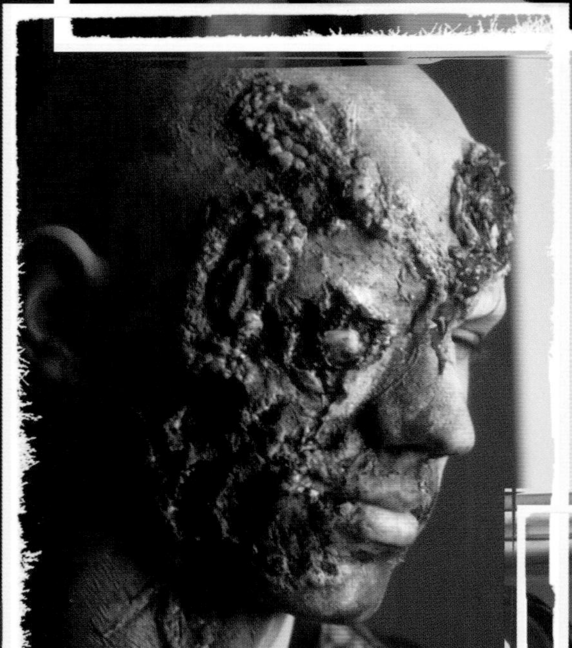

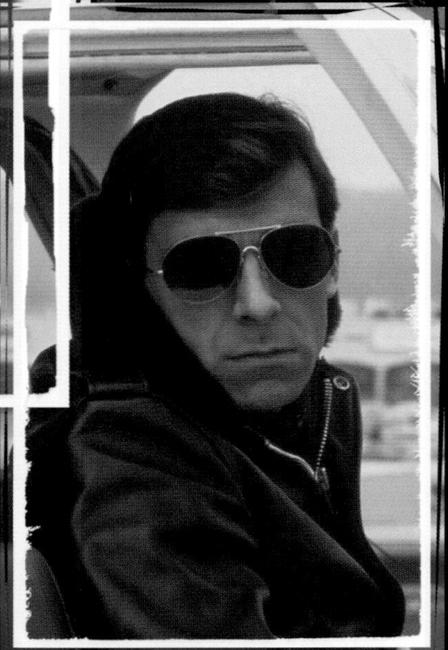

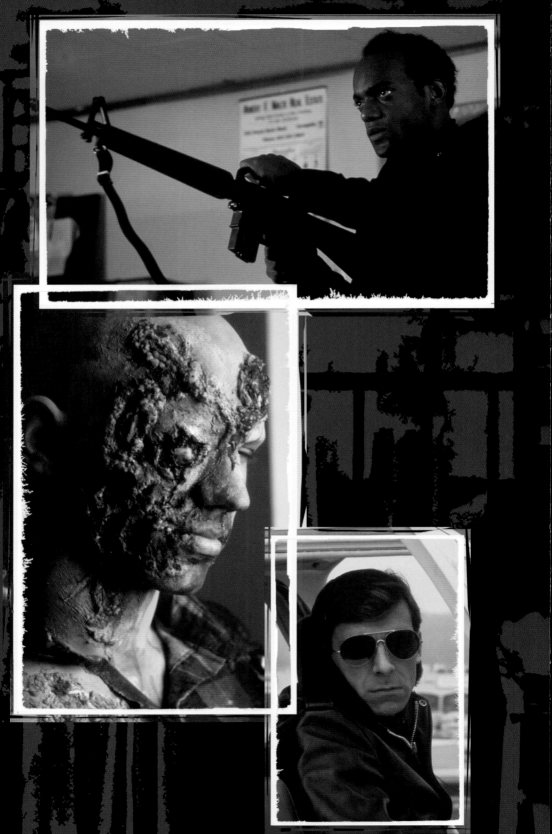

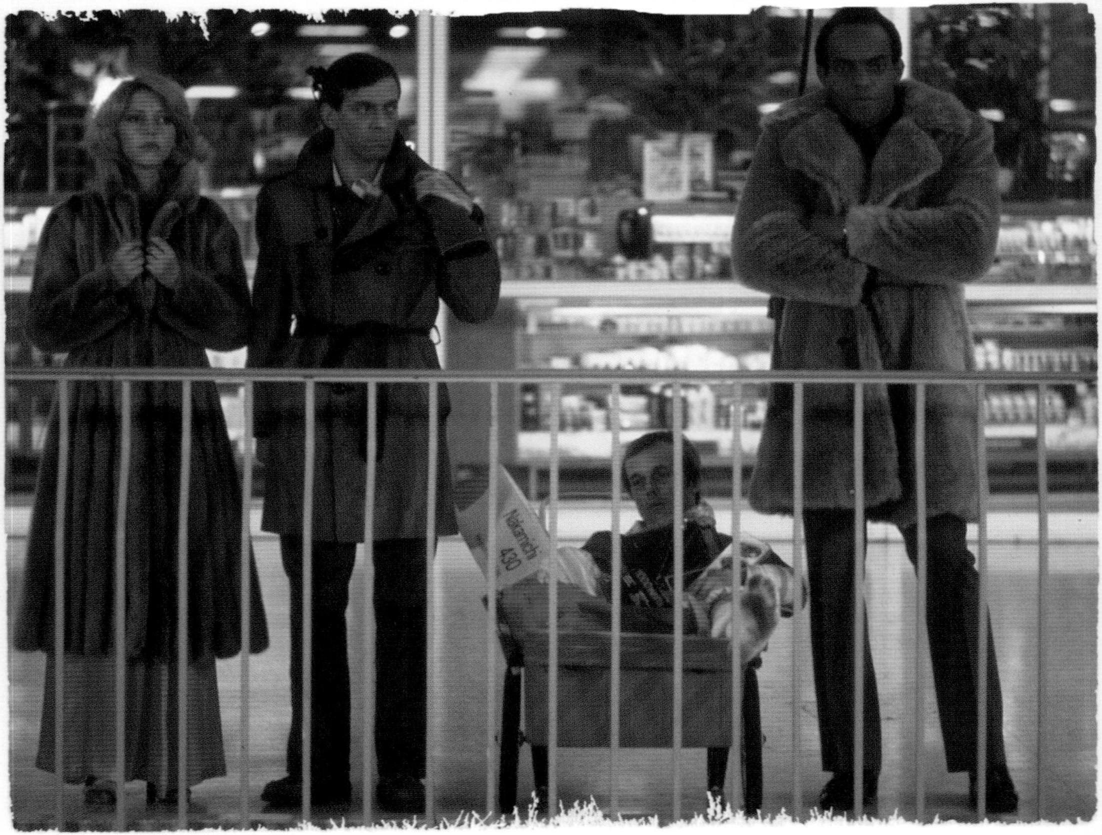
Nakamichi
430

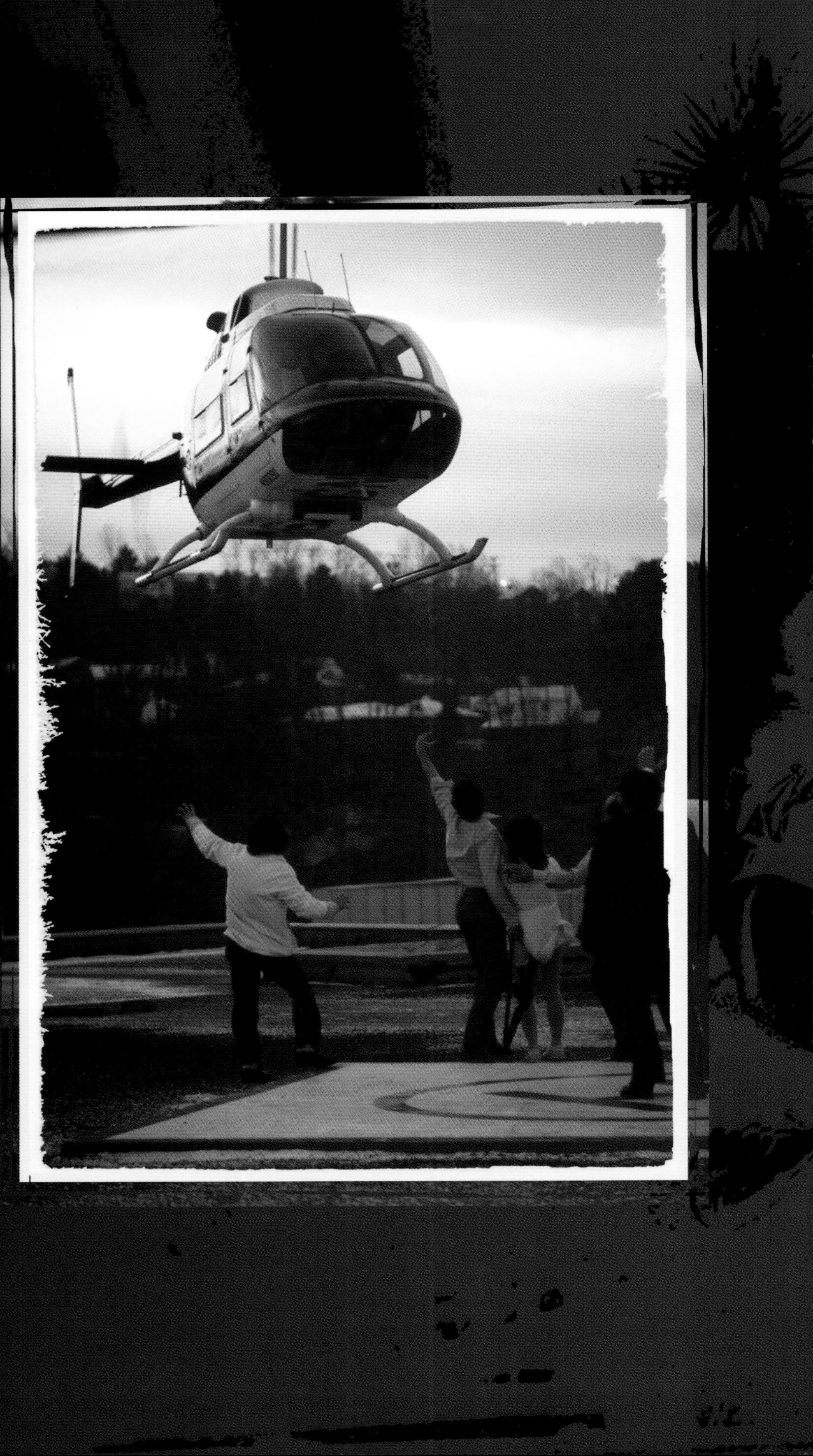

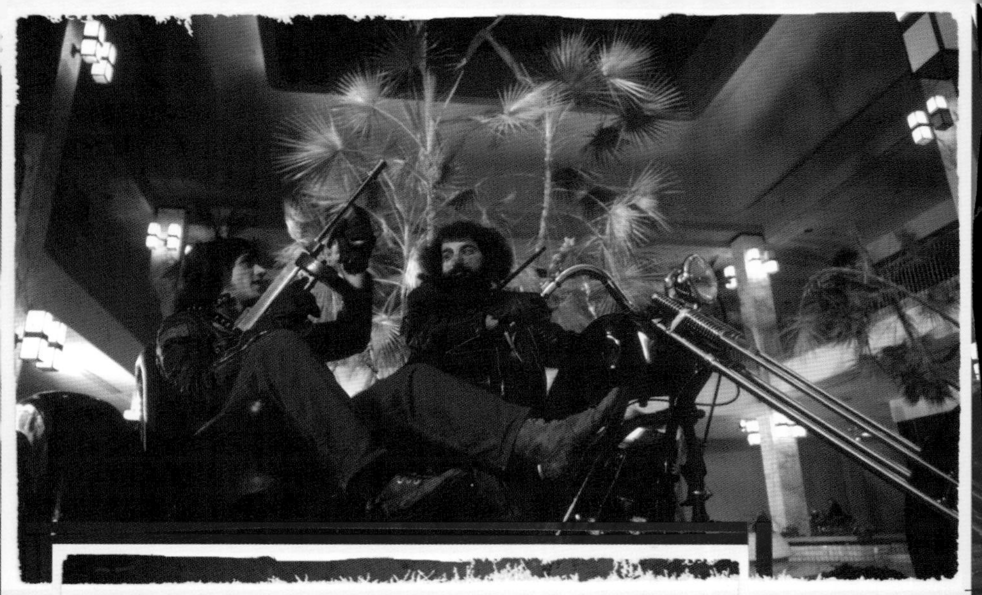
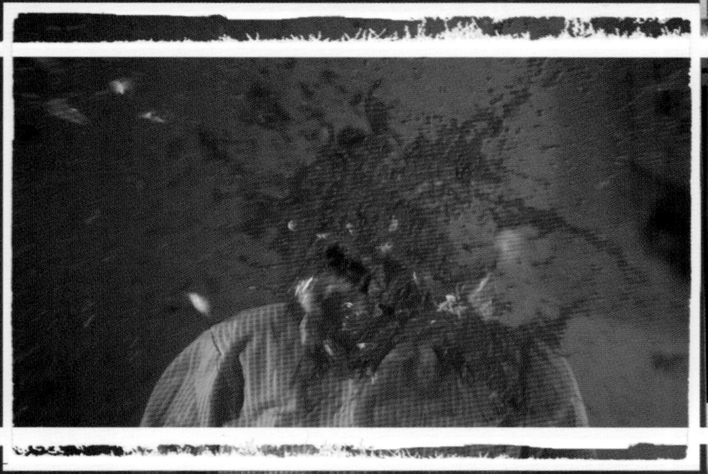
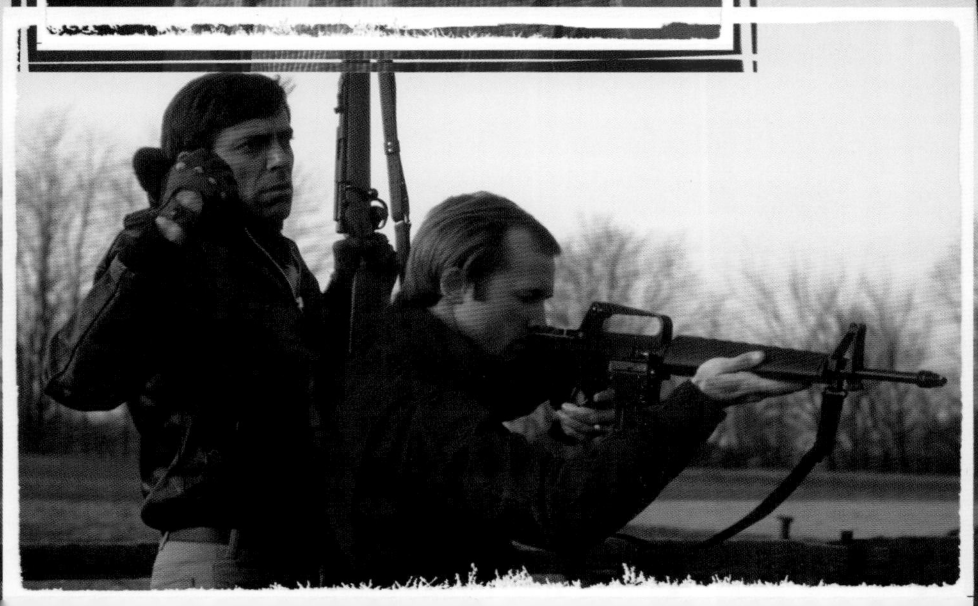

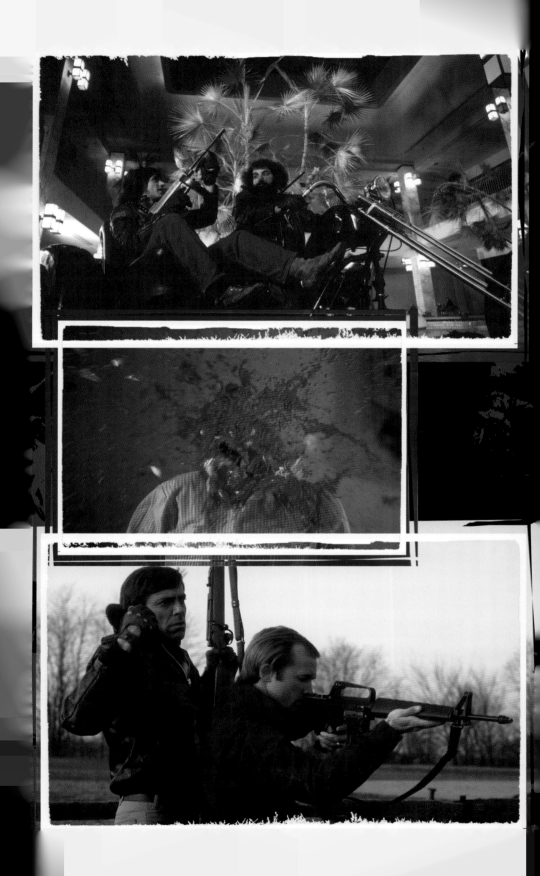

Books of interest from IDW Publishing

GRAPHIC NOVELS

CSI:
CRIME SCENE INVESTIGATION
BAD RAP

CSI: Bad Rap
Max Allan Collins
Gabriel Rodriguez/Ashley Wood
128 pages • $19.99
ISBN: 1-932382-20-8

CSI:
CRIME SCENE INVESTIGATION
serial

CSI: Serial
Max Allan Collins
Gabriel Rodriguez/Ashley Wood
144 pages • $19.99
ISBN: 1-932382-02-X

DAWN OF THE DEAD

George A. Romero's
Dawn of the Dead
Steve Niles/Chee
104 pages • $17.99
ISBN: 1-932382-32-1

SILENT HILL
DYING INSIDE

Silent Hill: Dying Inside
Scott Ciencin/Ben Templesmith
Aadi Salman/Ashley Wood
128 pages • $19.99
ISBN: 1-932382-24-0

DARK DAYS

Dark Days
Steve Niles/Ben Templesmith
144 pages • $19.99
ISBN: 1-932382-16-X

30 DAYS OF NIGHT

30 Days of Night
Steve Niles/Ben Templesmith
104 pages • $17.99
ISBN: 0-9719775-5-0

WAKE THE DEAD
STEVE NILES
CHEE

Wake the Dead
Steve Niles/Chee
128 pages • $19.99
ISBN: 1-932382-22-4

RICHARD MATHESON'S
I AM LEGEND

Richard Matheson's
I Am Legend
adapted by Steve Niles/Elman Brown
248 pages • HC • $35.00
ISBN: 1-932382-08-9

THE SHIELD
SPOTLIGHT

The Shield: Spotlight
Jeff Mariotte
Jean Diaz/Tommy Lee Edwards
128 pages • $19.99
ISBN: 1-932382-23-2

UNDERWORLD

Underworld
Kris Oprisko/Danny McBride
Nick Postic/Nick Marinkovich
144 pages • $19.99
ISBN: 1-932382-26-7

Spook house
Scott Hampton

Spookhouse: Book 1
Scott Hampton/Various
136 pages • $19.99
ISBN: 1-932382-15-1

THE BIBLE
EDEN

The Bible: Eden
Dave Elliott/Keith Giffen/Scott Hampton
104 pages • HC • $21.99
ISBN: 1-932382-13-5

NOVELS

GUNS, DRUGS, AND MONSTERS

Guns, Drugs and Monsters
Steve Niles/Ashley Wood
200 pages • $16.99
ISBN: 0-9719775-2-6

DIAL M FOR MONSTER

Dial M For Monster:
Cal McDonald Mystery Stories
Steve Niles/Various
200 pages • $16.99
ISBN: 1-932382-05-4

SAVAGE MEMBRANE

Savage Membrane
Steve Niles/Ashley Wood
200 pages • $16.99
ISBN: 0-9712282-3-X

THE SLAB
JEFF MARIOTTE

The Slab
Jeff Mariotte/
Tommy Lee Edwards
288 pages • $16.99
ISBN: 1-932382-07-0

www.idwpublishing.com

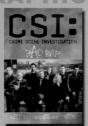

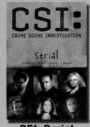

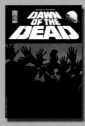

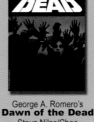

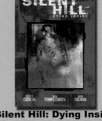

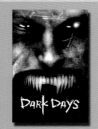

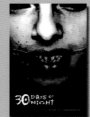

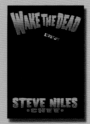

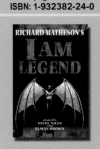

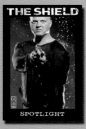

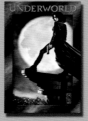

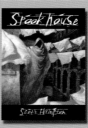

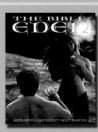

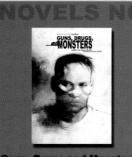

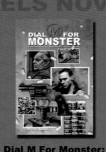

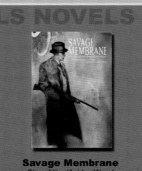

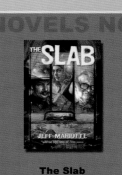

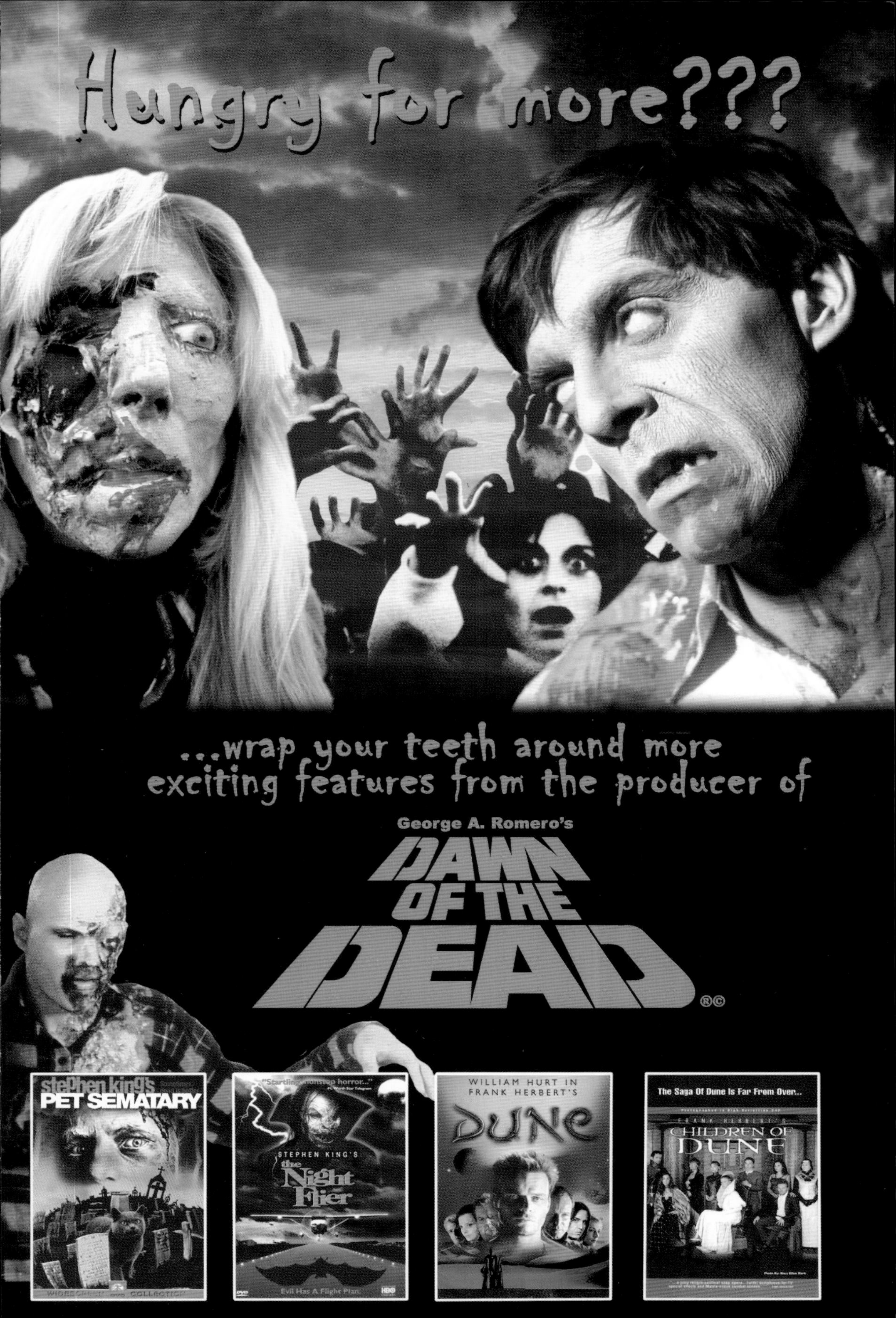
Hungry for more???
...wrap your teeth around more exciting features from the producer of
George A. Romero's
DAWN OF THE DEAD ®©
Stephen King's
PET SEMATARY
"Startling nonstop horror..."
STEPHEN KING'S
the Night Flier
Evil Has A Flight Plan.
WILLIAM HURT IN
FRANK HERBERT'S
DUNE
The Saga Of Dune Is Far From Over...
CHILDREN OF DUNE

a reading list
FROM
NEW AMSTERDAM ENTERTAINMENT, inc.

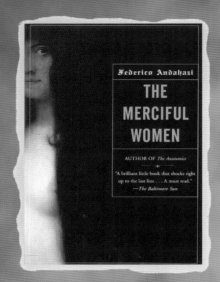

"This literary tour de force cum vampire tale will leave the reader gasping."
The Baltimore Sun

"Rich, complex, impossible to put down. From the imagination of Marge Piercy comes yet another stunning novel of morality and courage, a bold adventure of women, men, and the world of tomorrow."
The Boston Globe

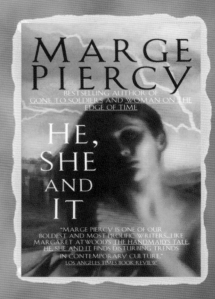

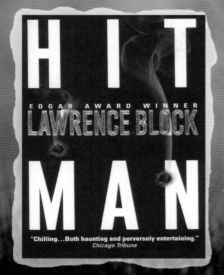

"Keller is the top of his class, an ace assassin. He may have no ethics, but he definitely has a way about him."
New York Times

"Fast-paced, insightful, and so suspenseful it zings like a high-tension wire."
Stephen King

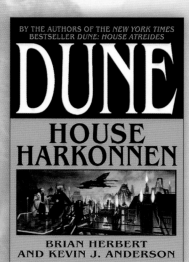

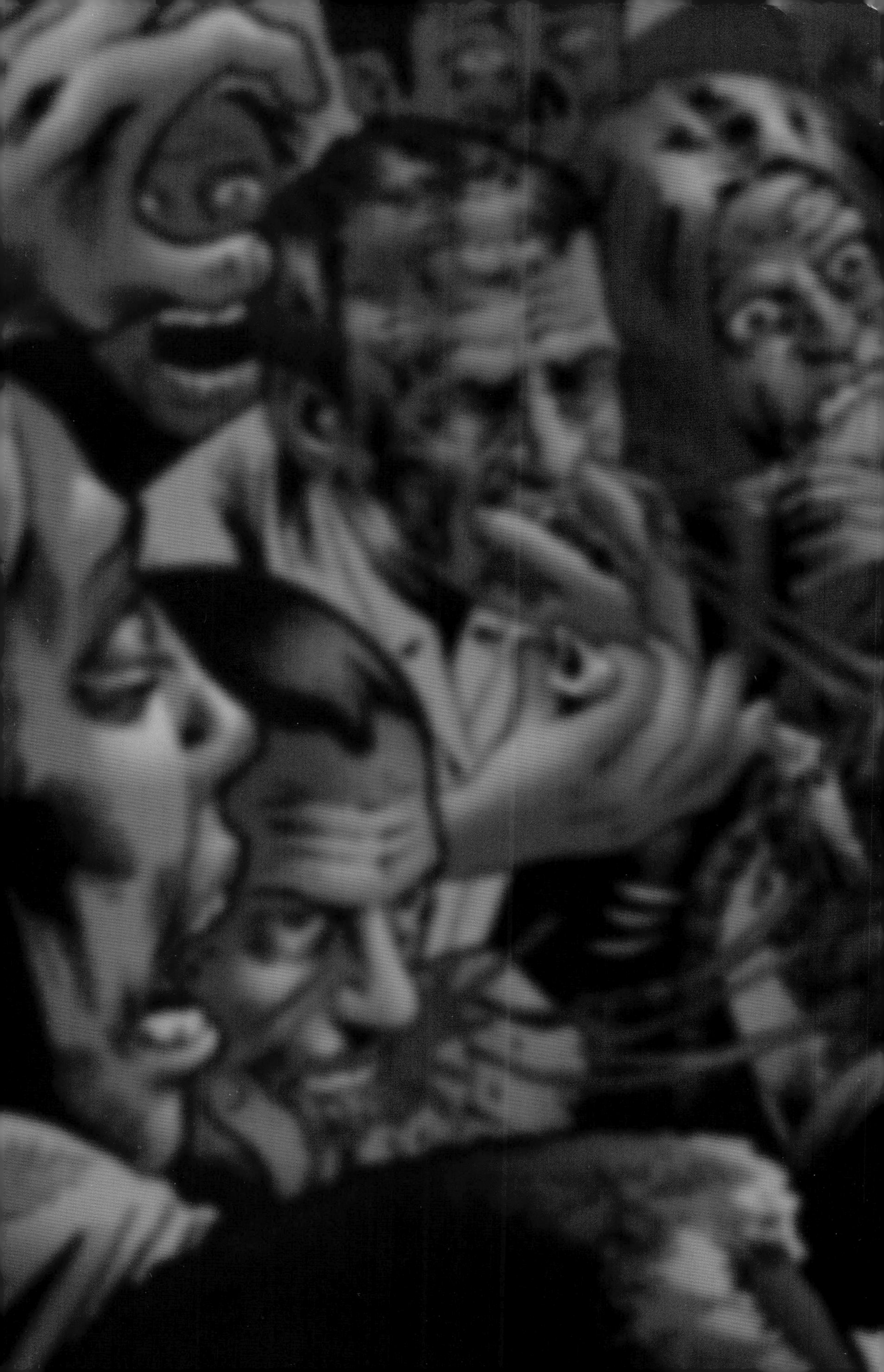